G000241018

Blood In, Blood Out

ART BLAJOS
WITH KEITH WILKERSON

SCB Publishers

MONARCH
Crowborough

British Library Cataloguing Data
A catalogue record for this book is available
from the British Library.

ISBN 1 85424 328 4

Co-published in South Africa with
SCB Publishers
Cornelis Struik House, 80 McKenzie Street
Cape Town 8001, South Africa.
Reg no 04/02203/06

*Front cover illustration by
Jimmy "Jimbo" Gutierrez*

Designed and produced by Bookprint Creative Services
P.O. Box 827, BN21 3YJ, England for
MONARCH PUBLICATIONS
Broadway House, The Broadway
Crowborough, East Sussex, TN6 1HQ.
Printed in Great Britain.

CONTENTS

Certain names have been changed in this true account of the author's life. In some instances, poetic license has been taken to combine multiple events and individuals' stories into combined climactic incidents for the sake of dramatic continuity.

Only by God's grace has Art Blajos been sent forth, a free man, to preach the Gospel and warn all who have ears to hear of the eternal and earthly consequences of choosing destructive and futile lives of crime. "If the Son therefore shall make you free, ye shall be free indeed," (John 8:36). All details of capital crimes within this book have been adapted from news accounts researched independently by the co-author, Keith Wilkerson.

"For the wages of sin is death; but the gift of God is eternal life through Jesus Christ our Lord" (Romans 6:23).

ACKNOWLEDGMENTS

I would like to acknowledge:

The greatest Man alive – my Lord Jesus Christ and his faithful servant, the Rev. Sonny Arguinzoni, my pastor and founder of Victory Outreach Ministries International.

I couldn't fairly mention all the men and women of Victory Outreach responsible for making this book a reality, but I would like to especially mention Simon Fox, Doreen Williamson and Kathy Clark. Without their effort and sacrifice, this book would not have been possible. And a special acknowledgment to the Arguinzonis, the Garcias, the Gonzaleses, the Clarks, the Villalobos, the Morenos, Joey Rosales, Richard "Cal" Almaraz and Joe and Rosalie Chavez. And last, but not least, the Blajos House. My love to you all.

In Christ,

ART BLAJOS
London, England

> *Jesus promises us all, "Behold I make all things new"*
> *(Revelation 21:5).*

FOREWORD

I was the director of the first Teen Challenge in Brooklyn, New York, when a skinny, strung-out heroin addict came stumbling in through the front door. This was the first time I laid eyes on Sonny Arguinzoni – the first person I ever discipled. Today I consider him my spiritual son.

That was back when Sonny and I were street kids. Now, many years later, Sonny is a pastor and I am an evangelist and our main thrust is sharing the love of Jesus with the misfits of society – children of the inner city.

Beginning with my miraculous conversion and then with Sonny's, the ripple effect of what God did in our lives is still being felt years later all around the world by all kinds of people.

Let me introduce you to Art Blajos.

Any visit to my close friend Sonny Arguinzoni's church in East Los Angeles is always an adventure. Recently, he pointed out one of the ushers. "That guy used to be a vicious criminal. No kidding. We've been reaching a lot of guys in the Mafia. We have one who was a hitman, Art Blajos. His testimony is so powerful that everybody who hears it knows that Jesus is real. The police even asked me, 'Is his conversion for real?' I told them, 'Oh, yes, he is genuine.'"

I have had the opportunity of meeting Art and hearing his incredible story.

Art was a sociopath, a social misfit. So much of his life was spent in prison and away from society. Art started reading the Bible while he was in a jail cell. He was supposed to kill the guy next to him there in the jail because the mob had a contract out on him. But after reading the Bible, somehow he could not kill him.

After Art got out of jail, he entered one of Victory Outreach's rehab homes and gave his life to Jesus. At first, he was very unemotional. He was like cold steel. Art committed so many conscience-killing acts that God had to do a resurrection to bring this "dead man walking" back from the dead so that he could function not only as a Christian, but even as a human being.

Gradually, he started breaking down as he felt acceptance and love and experienced the supernatural power of Jesus.

Now, he is a completely broken and repentant man with a tender heart.

In this powerful book, Art tells his whole, heart-breaking story. It is a tremendous testimony of what God can do with anybody – even Art Blajos. Even you. Even me.

Nicky Cruz
Colorado Springs, Colorado

INTRODUCTION

I'll never forget the day that Art came up to me with that chilling look of determination.

"Pastor," he said, "I have decided to be your back to back partner ... until death."

In my thirty years of Victory Outreach ministry, I have had a lot of young men come up to me, making a commitment to the ministry. Most of these young men were just grateful for being rescued from lifestyles of drug addiction and gang violence. I usually took their professions with a grain of salt. I knew time would tell.

But in Art's case I knew his commitment was different.

For the past ten years I have witnessed a profound miracle of God within Art's life. He came in one of the most hardened men I have ever known. His past involvement as a "Hitman" for one of the most feared prison gangs on the West Coast left an impression that at times would send a shiver down your back.

Then God began his transforming work.

Through the work of the Holy Spirit, Art has emerged as a trophy of God's grace. His testimony has given hope to thousands who are caught in situations where there seems to be no escape. The once feared hitman has become a wellspring of love and compassion.

I pray you will become inspired by the life of Art Blajos, from a young gang member on the streets of East Los Angeles to a mighty man of God who is ministering to hurting people around the world.

I am sure your life will not be the same after reading this book.

Sonny Arguinzoni

DEAD MAN WALKING

Shackled about my waist and ankles, I was escorted across the prison yard by two armed guards. Another guard stood on the wall above, rifle in hand.

"Dead man walking!" he shouted. It was a command to all the other prisoners to get out of my way. If they didn't, he would fire a warning shot.

The prisoners cleared a respectful path for me.

I shuffled through the crowd with my chains dragging on the ground, keenly aware that all eyes were fixed on me. The Brotherhood called out words of encouragement to me.

I knew what the other prisoners were thinking. I had witnessed other "dead men walking" many times.

I also knew that ordinary prisoners were in awe of me, for here was an accused murderer on trial for his life – a man who might soon die in the gas chamber. Some were also excited about being in the presence of such a dangerous criminal. They felt there was something heroic about me, as if I were a prisoner of war about to die at the hands of the enemy.

The guard called out again, "Dead man walking!"

"There's nothing dead about me," I muttered. "I'm *all the way alive*." But I couldn't deny the reality of my situation. It was as if I had the mark of Cain on my forehead. In the eyes of many, I was already condemned, doomed, destined for execution – with only my appointment in the gas chamber left to finish the story.

The State of California had raised me, fed me, housed me and clothed me since I was a mere boy, and now it wanted to kill me.

But the executioners were not the only ones with blood on their hands.

CHAPTER ONE
TIME FOR BLOOD

You might think that organized crime's assassins kill for money.

I didn't. I was accused of it – even prosecuted in a four-year trial that made the newspapers. They called me a murder-for-hire hit man. But I had a good lawyer and was acquitted.

During my long years in serious crime and in prison, some people did kill for money – it's not just a Hollywood myth. Maybe twenty per cent of the hits were for hire. But all the rest went down out of loyalty or to preserve respect.

If somebody was disloyal or disrespectful to the organization, he was killed for his offense against his brothers. His death served as an example for anybody who might be tempted to betray a sacred trust – such as ratting to the authorities or hijacking illegal drugs being delivered from one brother to another. Some deaths were motivated by inner-organization politics – favoritism or perhaps to eliminate some brother who knew dark secrets of the past or who was getting in good graces with a brother with powerful connections.

Let me tell you about Eddie Guzman. He had angered somebody. His name "was on *la lista*," as we said in Chino and Soledad and Tracy and Vacaville and San Quentin prisons – a hit list. His death had been ordered. In the movies, they say "there was a contract on his life".

There was no formal contract document ordering his death, just the word passed among brothers in and out of prison. He had to die. As a member of the Brotherhood, if I ran into him somewhere, I was under an obligation to snuff out his life.

I had been out of prison for a year, then I got arrested for drunk driving. The police had found tracks – needle marks – on my arm, evidence that I had been injecting heroin.

So they put me into a county jail for sixty days – long enough for me to kick my drug addiction, at least according to official policy. They, of course, did not acknowledge that drugs were just as plentiful inside as outside.

But I wanted to be drug free. Two months in jail would be an opportunity – a miserable one, but nevertheless an opportunity – to make it happen. Going through drug withdrawal is always a difficult thing, particularly in the liberty of what convicts call the "free world", life outside where everybody else lives. There, the temptations are strong, at least while you are concentrating on getting clean and sober.

Kicking drugs in jail is not so much easier. Steel bars force you to face reality.

Here, facing my need to be drug-free, I decided to go cold turkey.

I knew what to expect in this particular county jail. I had been there. I knew its chipped white bars and gray cement floors. The cells were tiny, five feet by nine feet.

New guys arrived in handcuffs and leg shackles, shuffling out of a dark and dusty sheriff's van that smelled of urine and vomit. Everything that had not already been taken away was placed in a basket.

You walk into a room wearing only what you came into the world with. There a guard in a bored voice makes you open your mouth, then let him look in your ears, lift your arms –and on down – as every body recess and cavity is examined routinely for contraband. It is very degrading. It is meant to be.

Then, still stripped, you walk to another room and are given prison clothes, which never fit right. As you walk out of processing, a group of glaring Black men in blue coverall jumpsuits huddle under a TV set, while several glaring Hispanics huddle under another.

There were calls of "Conejo" – my street gang nickname – as I was processed in. These were my friends. I shook their hands. I carried myself with a dark, reserved dignity. I watched carefully and saw that I was regarded with honor and admiration. I was a dangerous person capable of explosive violence. It was good that they already knew it. I did not have to establish myself here.

I was home.

Do not misunderstand me. Jail is a terrible place. Officials regulate when you eat, sleep, shower, exercise and sometimes even when you go to the bathroom. Freedom and liberty are left outside.

Prison is also an extremely dangerous place. You are mingling with people serving life sentences. What control does some guard with a night stick really have over someone serving three consecutive life sentences plus ninety-nine years, and who has accepted that he will never again touch a woman or wear civilian clothes or even be allowed to run? What do such people have to lose?

But I was used to living with the threat of violence twenty-four hours a day. I had developed the instincts to know when it was coming and how to survive it.

In this particular jail yard there were weight-lifting barbells, a dominoes table and several benches. Beyond were basketball hoops and an open-air handball court. Everything was behind chain-link fences topped with snarls of barbed wire as well as endless strands of *concertina*, razor-sharp metal looped atop the fences.

The loud din was oppressive. TV noise competed with radio chatter and the chaos of recorded music, all discordant with everything else. In the day room, TV sets were bolted to the ceiling, blaring whatever the guards were watching: soap operas in the afternoon and situation comedies during primetime, then old movies at night. Lots of people were talking. Some were yelling across the yards and inside the lockups. A few in their cells were screaming and arguing and throwing things. Nobody seemed to care. Over at a picnic table, there was a guy with a shaved head talking to nobody in particular.

Once before in this jail, there had been a young newcomer – new arrivals are called "fish" as in "a fish out of water." Just after his strip-search arrival, this fish was confronted in this very yard by a large former member of the Black Panthers who had crazy eyes. He said nothing, just smiled dangerously.

This fish had been in *juvie* – Juvenile Hall – and had graduated from that into the California Youth Authority, so he had an idea of what to expect. The fish clutched his armload of blankets and prison-issued clothes and followed after the guard. He made a show of making eye contact with friends he recognized from his neighborhood *cliqua*, the notorious First Flats gang. They nodded back.

Later in the lunchtime chow line, the former Black Panther fell in behind the new kid. The older guy was a weight-lifter – big and bald with no neck. His name was Sick Rick. He kept smiling and offering to help.

That afternoon, the new guy returned to his cell and on his bunk were a carton of cigarettes and a set of prison blues – shirt and pants – nicely folded, starched and creased. Thinking this was a gift from his homeboys from the First Flats, he went down the tier and thanked them.

They stared at him in silence.

One of them said it wasn't from them.

Again they watched him in silence – waiting to see what he was going to do.

The new kid didn't like it. He did not like the disrespect he was receiving. He did not like the fear he was feeling. He put the carton of cigarettes on a bunk. "I need a blade," he said.

Nobody said anything.

In the silence, one of the guys reached out and took the cigarettes. "*Orale, carnal,*" he said in slang Spanish. "Lemme see what is going on, *ese.*"

At supper, the newcomer was again befriended by Sick Rick.

The kid tensed.

He tried not to respond.

The threat against him was serious and real — and night-time was falling. Some inmates have never known a woman or have accepted the fact that due to their long sentences, they will never touch a female again. Many such inmates are not effeminate. They are twisted, predatory, often vicious, enjoying sex only if it happens after a long, perverse seduction. Many want rape — with their victim resisting, terrorized and whimpering for help that will not come.

A young convict must be wary of strangers and friendship. One of the oldest tricks around is for a young new guy to be befriended by a longtimer, often a lifer, who gives him candy and drugs — and cigarettes and nicely starched blues. After several days or weeks of gifts, the lifer asks for a favor — usually sexually related. When the new kid refuses, the longtimer gives him an account of all the candy and cigarettes and other gifts and demands payment. Either the kid can pay up or submit.

Of course, the longtimer has carefully waited until the bill is high enough that the kid doesn't have that kind of money. Then the interest payments start. The kid starts paying every cent that he can get relatives to send in. But it is never enough. Eventually, the kid is given a new choice — submit or be killed. A lot of the suicides in prison are actually murder. A kid will be found hanging by his bedsheets. What is not reported is that he was hung there by people holding his arms and legs until he was no longer breathing.

The new kid carefully stared ahead, trying to show no fear or weakness.

But he knew he had to move.

His friends were watching him. They knew what was happening. But nobody said anything.

When he got back to his cell, he saw an extra blanket on his bunk. He unfolded it warily. Inside the folds, he found an eight-inch homemade knife. He slipped it into his waistband.

That evening he walked across the lighted yard toward his

friends. Sick Rick was bench-pressing 200 pounds over at the pile of weights.

The new kid stared straight ahead, his face expressionless.

"*Carnales,* I got no choice," he said to his friends. "I have to move on that *mayate*. All I want you to do is watch my back. Just cover me. Make sure that none of his people try to hit me from the back."

"*Orale,*" answered one of the kids from First Flats — slang for "OK."

The newcomer casually walked towards the weights. Sick Rick was sweating and grunting, pumping iron and staring at the darkening sky. A tall black guy was spotting for him — standing by his head, ready to help lift the weights if Rick couldn't press them heavenward one more time.

The Hispanic newcomer looked around. His homeboys — friends from his neighborhood — sauntered around the yard, positioning themselves beside the right people. A big kid from the First Flats stepped around behind Sick Rick's spotter, who turned, concerned that someone was at his back.

Like lightning, the newcomer moved. Sick Rick exhaled in surprise as the 200 pounds he was benchpressing came down hard on his chest. In the same instant, eight inches of sharpened steel penetrated his heart. Six times in mere seconds the crude blade flashed in and out.

Sick Rick's spotter spun, stunned at the speed of the new guy's attack. He said nothing. It was too late. The kid was walking away. So were the kid's homeboys.

In the next confused moments, shots were being fired, whistles were blowing and in the blare of "all inmates return to your cells immediately," the young newcomer was strolling nonchalantly back to his cell after passing off the bloody knife.

Sick Rick was dead.

There would be an investigation, but no case, which means no one ratted — not even Sick Rick's spotter or other friends. Dramatically, boldly, the new kid had established himself. The smooth-faced 19-year-old was no longer a fish.

He was unquestionably someone who would be given a wide berth.

It was whispered that he had killed many times before. *He should be respected.*

Nobody else would ever disrespect him without very careful calculation.

"Why do we have to wear these dumb-looking jumpsuits?" another newcomer asked that first day as I stepped out into the yard.

"It makes you a better target," I replied.

"That's not funny," said the new guy.

"It wasn't meant to be," said an expressionless guard.

Eddie Guzman was only in this jail temporarily – being held pending resolution of charges.

He was scared, I could tell. He was a slender man in his late 30s. He laid on his bed and read a Bible, pushing his black, wire-rimmed glasses up on his nose. He seldom came out of his cell.

He looked worried. He had every right to be. He was condemned, but not by the courts. He was only awaiting trial and could have been released at any time, particularly if the prosecutor dropped charges for lack of evidence or because of too heavy a caseload.

But Eddie, everyone knew, was doomed. What had he done to deserve death? I had no idea.

Perhaps he had robbed a 14-year-old runner – a drug delivery kid – and had taken cocaine that had belonged to somebody in the Brotherhood, maybe a major dealer in the organization. If that was the case, Eddie had set his own execution.

Or maybe he had gotten somebody else's action – partying with the girlfriend of somebody influential.

It could have been that he knew where important bodies were buried. That can be fatal. It is never wise to let people know that you know too much.

His rendezvous with death began when he was arrested on suspicion of holding up a liquor store. The judge who denied his bail probably had no idea he was giving Eddie a death sentence. Or maybe he did know. Sometimes the authorities made their moves with calculation. Sometimes they used the forces that ran the jails for their own purposes.

No matter what state you are talking about authorities rarely have complete control of the jails – not completely. You might think that the guards always run a jail or that the warden calls the shots. Not so.

There is a constant power struggle. Convicts are amazingly inventive. Toilets can be turned into telephones – remove the water and the plumbing pipes become an intercom. Also, there are ways to pass drugs and contraband from one tier to another through the toilets by using strips of sheets tied together.

In my young adulthood, the power was divided between the Black Family – who were primarily African-American Muslims, and the White Supremacists – neo-Nazi white guys, *la Clika,* and the Brotherhood of which I was a member.

In order to maintain peace, officials in most states segregate the rival groups – for example, Hispanics on one tier, the White Supremacists on another, then the Black Family on another. When I was in prison, if guards wanted to get rid of a troublemaker, they could move him onto the wrong tier, intentionally. There his execution was just a matter of time – for purely gang-warfare reasons, nothing personal.

I was almost killed that way once when I took a guard hostage. One of my brothers had been murdered by a rival gang and I had it all worked out where a few of us were going to do a hit-and-run up on their tier and take some quick, deadly revenge. Unfortunately, the whole thing fell apart and I ended up holding a guard in my cell.

I found myself sent to a block where my cell was surrounded by BF members who did not consider me anything remotely resembling their brother. Racial threats were whispered constantly. Everybody passing my cell was my potential killer.

I did not cower. I showed them no weakness and no fear. I stayed moves ahead of them – such as keeping a towel nearby in case somebody threw a smoke bomb into my cell to suffocate me. I could stick my head into the bowl of the toilet and flush it over and over, breathing into my lungs the relatively clean air from the sewer pipes so that I did not die from the choking smoke of my burning cell.

I survived. Try to understand the special determination that it took not only to make it through such an ordeal, but to emerge feared and respected.

Even back on the Brotherhood tier among my friends, no one's safety was guaranteed. In prison, an offense requiring death could be small – such as laughing too much with the wrong people or balking at an order by a high-ranking gang member. Respect is important. Showing weakness hurts everybody. Whoever stabs the traitor, sending him into eternity does it as a favor and an honor.

Losers in powerplays do not live either. No one retires from being the top guy. He is killed. "Blood in, blood out," goes the phrase describing how to get in and out of the Brotherhood.

You only got into the Brotherhood – which during my young adulthood dominated the Californian prisons – by being permitted to remove an enemy of the gang from his earthly existence. If you were approved for acceptance, you got an assignment to send an enemy to hell. If you did, you were virtually guaranteed acceptance into the family.

No money was involved. That would degrade the whole thing.

We're talking loyalty, and power, and, of course, respect. Yeah, and a little greed. But mostly respect.

Nobody is going to cross your hand with $100,000 like in the movies – nor $10 for that matter. Your *carnales*, or brothers, have good money – from drugs and robbery and extortion, you name it. And if you are behind bars, you take care of family business out of gratitude that your brothers on the outside are making sure that your wife and kids and mother do not starve.

Money is being provided to them.

And when you get out, you will take care of the family needs of those you left inside. But you do not kill so that your old lady will get a suitcase full of drug money.

No, it is just the opposite. Because you are a part of a close-knit brotherhood, you know that she will not be abandoned on the streets. You do not have to go crazy worrying about her – driving yourself psychotic as you endure hard time behind steel bars. Instead, you know she is OK. So, you keep your mind on business, like getting out or running drugs inside the prison or seeing that rats do not live.

Again, do not misunderstand. Your children, if you have them, are branded – their father is a jailbird. Of course, in certain circles, this gives them special status, enjoying a certain admiration that their dad is such a dangerous person. But life is not easy for them. Your enemies are targeting your house, since it is a way to get back at you for any offense of the past. One great way to disrespect an enemy is to steal his woman. In jail, you can do nothing about it. Except wait. And plot vengeance.

In this county jail I was relatively safe. I was respected. I was divorced from my wife and did not care particularly what happened to her. Here, I was known.

Here I would kick my heroin addiction – of which I was personally ashamed. For about ten days I knew I would suffer with sleeplessness and a terrible aching, gnawing craving for the illegal power that I had used to instantly ease everything wrong in the world. As my emptiness grew, my symptoms would grow worse – diarrhea, vomiting, extreme irritability. Nothing would be right. Everything would be terrible – and the urge would be to confront anyone who crossed me with violent rage.

But I wanted to be drug-free. I'd been having dreams about being totally clean and sober, starting my life all over in Arizona maybe – perhaps out in the desert.

But complicating my plan was this guy named Eddie in the very next cell to me. Drug withdrawal or not, it was my obligation to kill him before he was out of reach – released on bail or taken to court.

As I sat on my bunk, feeling the first tremors of drug withdrawal, I focused on killing him. You do not just snuff somebody without careful planning. You stalk them. You seduce them. I had to plan everything very, very carefully so that there would be no proof that I was the one who executed him. As I laid there, I walked through every step of my murder plan a hundred times in my head.

Within hours of my arrival, I had gotten a homemade knife passed to me for the purpose at hand. It was known what I had to do.

Now I tried to figure an angle to get close to him. I hit on the idea of using his religion since he was always reading a Bible. I yelled over to him and asked what he was doing. He didn't answer at first, then told me that he was reading Psalms.

I played poker-face with him – making a game of winning him over. I had done it before. I was good at seducing my victims – like a spider and a fly – so they never knew what was up, never suspecting they were about to be done in or that I was the one to do it.

I liked to get close emotionally to a hit. I would be their friend. I would hear their troubles and complain about the same injustices that we both were enduring – bad food, cold cells, the foul stench and the unending, penetrating noise that drives some inmates mad. It is never quiet in prison.

Eventually, we would pledge to watch out for each other. In this particular county jail, inmates in our cellblock were allowed to shower only on Saturday mornings – and even then it was up to the inmate. Jailhouse showers can be a dangerous place, so some seldom go. They just sponge off in their cell. You can imagine the body odor of the more paranoid guys who will not risk leaving their cells. They get pretty rank.

I knew the showers would be the best time to hit Eddie. Since showering was not mandatory, though, I would have a far better chance of carrying out the hit – and getting away with it – if I got him to trust me. I had to get him to relax and confide in me.

I had to wait for the right opportunity.

When it finally came time to shower, I would need to have worked things just right so that he would feel at ease with me there watching his back. Only then, I knew, would he come out of his cell on Saturday morning, laughing and talking to me.

In the shower, as he closed his eyes to shampoo his hair, I would thrust a steel shank into his heart and push his face down into the shower drain. I would watch his hands unclench lifelessly there under the running water as other inmates walked away. I would press his mouth against the concrete floor, silent in his last, unheard cry.

Then I would be gone.

When the guards found him, no one would know what had happened or who had been with him nor how long he had been dead.

If I changed my mind and did not kill him, I would brand myself as hesitant and weak. The Brotherhood does not tolerate weakness. If it did, discipline would crumble. Respect would fade. The fear that holds everything together would collapse.

So I had little choice. It was him or me. Eddie had to die.

But first I had to gain his trust. There in the cell, as I was going through cold turkey, I started talking with him about his Bible. I passed hours with him, listening to his religious talk, then telling him lies about my old lady. A few in the cell block were waiting, watching, knowing what was going down. Most did not.

As my withdrawal intensified, I paced up and down in my cell, smoking cigarettes, trying to tough-out the pain, talking with Eddie, gaining his trust like a cobra seduces a mouse.

Around midnight, Eddie called my name. "Hey, Conejo, look

over here," he called. Since the cells were separated by solid walls, I had to use a little hand mirror to see him. I held it outside my bars and angled it so I could look into his cell.

There was Eddie sitting on the edge of his bed with a tourniquet on his arm, injecting cocaine. I knew it was coke because the liquid in the syringe was clear. If it had been heroin, it would have been dark brown.

"Do you want some, Conejo?" he asked.

"No," I said. "You're weak taking that stuff." I really didn't want any. Plus, he only had a little – certainly not enough for both of us.

As he eased the coke into his vein, he jerked with the ecstasy of the rush. Then he said to me, "You know what, Conejo? Jesus Christ can change your life."

That made me very mad.

All his religious talk before had just been amusing. But now, with a needle in his vein, it was sacrilegious. If I could have reached him, I would have snuffed him right there – unconcerned that the evidence would convict me. He was shooting stolen coke in front of me while I was hurting and he was mocking me by coming across like some holy missionary of Christian mercy.

It turned my stomach.

I thought that for some reason he was trying to play on me his jailhouse salvation con, "the Jesus Game," making a big show out of being converted and transformed so the authorities would send him out into the free world and preach to sinners to turn from their wicked ways. Prisoners make such pleas to judges and wardens and counselors. Remarkably, it works some of the time. You just have to be a good enough actor.

I was unimpressed, however. It was just one more con job.

"No, really, man," exclaimed Eddie, slumping back on his bunk, his face flushed with the drug rush. "Jesus Christ is absolutely, uh, you know, real, man." He sighed – his mind drifting elsewhere.

So I hid my intense anger and answered him in a friendly voice, "Hey, homeboy, tell me about Jesus."

He looked kind of blank, then squinted. His eyes danced. He smiled at me blissfully. "Say what?"

I wanted him to think I was getting weak and becoming religious. "I want to know more, man," I said. "You make it seem so real."

"Oh, yeah," he whispered. "Like God, you know…"

I was so angry. I could feel the knife in my hand. I wanted to slide it in between his ribs and smell the stench of death and feel him fight futilely against the blade. He had dared to disrespect me with this Jesus game. He had seriously misjudged me. I was a habitual criminal with a multiple-page rap sheet of convictions, arrests, and suspected offenses, but I was a straightforward guy and I demanded that people be straight with me. I didn't want to be sucked into their jailhouse con jobs.

Eddie started getting a buzz. I half-listened while he rattled on about godly salvation. He talked about Revelation. He talked about Babylonians. He talked about some dude named Stephen getting stoned.

After a while, I had to interrupt him. "Hey, man," I said, "if this Jesus is looking out for you, then how come you're in this place?"

"Because I'm a backslider," he said.

"What is that?"

"A backslider is a Christian who has stopped going to church, stopped reading his Bible, stopped praying. Eventually, he ends up going back to the filth he came from. That's what happened to me. It's my fault I'm in here, because I turned my back on Jesus. I went back to doing armed robberies and coke."

My withdrawal symptoms were getting worse. I don't think I heard most of what the guy was saying.

As it got late, I began what I feared would be a really bad night. As he talked on and on about God, I paced back and forth in my cell in pain, craving heroin. I was deeply aware of the futility of my life. Here I was in jail once again. I had already spent more than half of my life behind bars.

Ever since I had been 14 years old, I had been in and out of places like this. I knew that if I was sloppy in killing Eddie on Saturday morning, I could even end up in the gas chamber. The way I was feeling, I might not cover my crime very well. I might leave a key, tell-tale piece of evidence. I might not kill him instantly – instead leaving him alive to tell who had done it.

As I lay on my bunk, my stomach in nervous knots, my head spinning, my mind in depression, I knew that if for some reason they only let us go to the showers two at a time, I would be the only suspect.

But as I wrestled with my torment, I was determined that I had to do my duty and kill this lying hypocrite.

It was my duty to my brothers.

Plus, I was tired of hearing his mouth.

Excitedly jabbering away in the cell next to me, this coke fiend went on and on talking about how much he loved the dear Jesus Christ. He got more and more hyper and animated as the night stretched on.

"I used to have a nice home, a good wife, a great job and I used to go to church," he was telling me in the darkness.

"So," I yelled, "how come this Jesus didn't stop you from coming to jail?"

"As long as I was obeying him, he protected me. I was off drugs for a long time. People warned me about how easy it was to slide back into being a junkie, but I didn't listen."

I jumped up and began pacing off my cold sweats. I hurt all over. I was trembling. I was fighting it off by weighing my options. If I got caught for killing Eddie, I might be here another ten or twenty years. Or I might be executed.

Or I could let Eddie live. That would mean my own certain death. If I did not kill Eddie, my brothers, whose cause I had spent years upholding and defending, would execute me as an example for showing weakness. And for disobeying.

I squatted on the cold floor and rubbed my arms. I was freezing. I was hit with a sudden clarity that my life was and always had been just a lie. I had been living a massive deception. All the talk about brotherhood and family was just lies. In reality, my crime family was a ruthless, vicious, dog-eat-dog power struggle. As long as a brother was strong, he could survive, but as soon as he began to weaken or wanted out, he was a dead man.

Nobody got out alive. So much for crime "family loyalty."

My stomach convulsed as I rocked on my feet, my fists clenched. Eddie kept babbling on. My head pounded. My bones ached. Wracked with a sudden wave of nausea, I vomited my supper onto the concrete floor. My pain was so raw that I couldn't sit. I couldn't lie down. I could only squat and pace and smoke cigarettes and walk back and forth in my cell like a caged animal.

At about three in the morning, Eddie shut up. He was lying on his bunk with a beatific smile, sleeping like a baby. I hated him. I knew I was going to enjoy killing him. His blood would drip from the homemade knife waiting now under my pillow. His blank eyes would gawk in lifelessness, then roll back. And I would walk away emotionless.

My knife would disappear as happens in prison. No inmates would be able to remember who had gone into the shower at the same time as the dead guy.

And my family's honor would be protected. Another stiff in the morgue would testify to the mortal folly of betraying the Brotherhood.

And I would be out of jail in just a few days, free as a bird – and clean of heroin.

I held my mirror out to see if Eddie really was sleeping. I noticed that a Bible was sitting on the bars – as if he had left it there for me. I decided to read some of it to take my mind off my withdrawal pain. I liked reading – I had always read a lot in prison, but mostly books on power and struggle. As I grabbed it, I was trembling.

"I ain't afraid of a Bible!" I said to convince myself.

I opened it up. The pages crackled as I turned them – in the relative silence of the early morning, it seemed loud. I froze and made sure that no one had heard. I started reading the book of Acts, all about a guy named Saul.

He was a killer. He had been on a journey to a place called Damascus where he intended to execute a lot of Christians. Just my kind of guy. Then he was thrown off his feet right there in the road and he saw a great light. A voice said to him, "Saul, Saul, why are you persecuting me?"

"Who are you, Lord?" asked Saul – as if he didn't know.

"I am Jesus, whom you are persecuting."

I read on, and it seemed like a good story. I read for hours, going right through Acts. It gripped me. I admired Saul's loyalty and commitment to the cause he believed in. He had been an executioner of Christians.

Then, he became a bold defender of the Brotherhood – the Christian Brotherhood.

I liked him.

He was the first Bible character I had ever been able to take seriously. I had heard about David and Goliath, and Noah's Ark, and Jonah and the whale. I thought those were just kids' stories. This was different – this Saul impressed me.

I went back and read where he helped kill the Stephen dude who got stoned.

I woke up to the sound of knocking on the bars of my cell. A food tray was pushed under the bars. I had been asleep, perhaps for hours. I checked to make sure that the Bible was out of sight – good, it was hidden under my blanket. Then it suddenly dawned on me – I had been asleep! How could that be? When you're going through withdrawal you don't sleep – not for at least ten days. And I felt hungry too, so I started to eat. But that was impossible – I should have been unable to eat because of stomach cramps. I figured that maybe I just had a strong constitution. As I ate the food and drank the coffee, I felt good.

In fact, I felt great!

For some reason even the guard looked friendly to me. His uniform looked sharp, his attitude seemed respectful. Everything looked good. He asked me, "Are you coming out?"

My defenses went up. Why would he ask that? Why did he care? Was he part of a hit? Was somebody after me?

Reality hit me like a brick – it was Saturday morning! It was time to shower.

In the next cell, Eddie was coming out for his shower.

I grabbed my towel. I reached under my pillow for my knife. A bunch of other guys were walking down the ramp. My perfect opportunity was here. A lot of guys would be in the shower. They would cover for me. My mind was completely clear. Soon Eddie would be a corpse testifying to the folly of doublecrossing our Brotherhood. This is enough reason.

I stepped outside. Eddie smiled and walked just ahead of me, trembling and weak, but looking back for support. I nodded. He draped his towel over his shoulders. He knew I was watching his back.

I caught knowing glances from the other inmates. They were going to see his blood flow.

I walked down the corridor. I held my blade under my towel – out of sight. Eddie suspected nothing. Just as I had planned, he had been completely reassured by our conversations.

Whenever I was about to strike a victim, I made sure that I never looked in their eyes. I would just look at the target where I was going to thrust the blade. Calmly, I talked with Eddie to keep him at ease.

The moment was coming.

The guard stepped away.

Steam rose from the shower room. I followed Eddie in. He put his head back under a stream of water. I started to whirl around and strike him in the heart, but then I did something I had never done before: *I looked at his eyes.*

When I did, I felt something hit me like a wave. Somehow I

saw Eddie as a human being – as a person, not just a target.

He was *alive*. I was going to *end* it all for him – something he did not deserve. Such second thoughts had never bothered me before. I had always been able to switch off my emotions and just take care of business.

Eddie stared at me.

He knew what was happening. He was paralyzed by fear. His face went white. He stared at me, transfixed, like a terrified little mouse. He did not resist. In the next seconds, he would be dead, his face in the drain. Everyone would step out as if nothing had happened. They would return to their cells as I mixed in with them. The knife would disappear. Nobody would be blamed for the dead man in the shower.

It was time for blood. He was mine!

It was time.

But I did not move.

If I did not kill him, I would be dead in hours.

I clutched the knife.

I stared into Eddie's terrified eyes.

CHAPTER TWO

MY DISCONNECTED CHILDHOOD

On the streets, we called ourselves the Brotherhood.

Some people say that more than 500 gangs, with some 80,000 known members, infest Los Angeles County. I have heard higher numbers as well as lower. A recent district attorney's report said that there are 125,000 to 130,000 gang members in the county, but that a distinction must be made between active, hard-core gang members and anyone who ever hung out with gang members, or was arrested once as a juvenile in the company of gang members, or even briefly flirted with joining a gang before pulling back.

The reality of life in a gang-infested neighborhood is that every boy and girl must by necessity associate with gang members, because gang members are their classmates, their neighbors, their relatives. Often their fathers and grandfathers have tattoos from their own days in the local gang.

Gang-related homicides in Los Angeles have risen steadily, from 212 in 1984 to 803 in 1992. There are as many as 3,000 gang-related murders nationwide each year, according to some experts. Many of the hits are committed by young kids.

I have been there.

I have been there – feeling no remorse, graduating from a stiletto .22 revolver to a .38 semi-automatic.

I have basked in the respect that my reputation earned me. Cops, gang members, shopkeepers and social workers in East Los Angeles describe their communities as "war zones" these days. I grew up in those trenches when today's war was just beginning.

My father was Greek. I don't know if he knew what a rough time I was having as a 9-year old. If he did, he didn't do anything about it.

He was actually half-Greek and half-Mexican, living in the gringo world that is Southern California. I don't know if anybody ever called him "Griego," the Spanish word for "Greek" from which "gringo" supposedly comes.

He certainly didn't look like an "Anglo," the more polite term for outsiders – which actually means "English". We big-city Chicano kids turned no other cheek. Given our Latin blood and culture, we let no insult – real or imagined – go unchallenged and certainly no disrespect unanswered. We were proud and very poor. We defended our great pride with our fists. And our pool cues.

Billiards was one of my dad's favorite occupations. He was not a pool hustler. He was an upholsterer until he had to depend more on pool than upholstering for income after arthritis set in, brought on by an injury to his right hand during a family brawl.

With his jet-black hair and Mediterranean complexion, my father, George Blajos, looked as Hispanic as any of my uncles or cousins, except for his deep blue eyes. Those piercing European eyes attracted the ladies, who always caught his gaze. Even in the middle of a billiards shot, my dad would pause – distracted by the flash of a feminine smile.

Family was important when I was young. Belonging to a large and loving clan of emotional, expressive and basically good people gave me what little security I did have as a motherless little boy.

My mom had been a beautiful woman. That was all my father ever chased – great beauties.

You might think it is corny but I can close my eyes and imagine them in love, him carrying her across the threshold after a traditional, Mexican wedding at the altar of a small Catholic church. I can see him, stocky and muscular in all of his five feet eight inches with my mother clutching his neck and laughing into his eyes.

But I can only imagine romantic scenes like that.

I never saw them in love.

I only knew them at each other's throats – accusing, demanding, refusing to take custody of my big brother, Ernie, and me – screaming threats at one another, vowing to get even. Her name was Lupe – named after Mexico's patron saint, the Virgin of Guadalupe, who appeared before a simple Indian peasant, according to the legend that every Mexican child knows, declaring that the God of the conquering and enslaving Europeans who were overrunning Mexico actually loved the defeated Aztec people.

They were my people. I was born Arthur George Blajos five minutes after midnight on November 2, 1950 at Los Angeles County Hospital – a US citizen. When I was still a baby, my mother left us. She loaded up all our family's furniture, then put 3-year-old Ernie and me on the porch. She drove away, leaving the two of us to wait for my father to come home.

We were discovered by uncles or cousins or somebody – maybe after the neighbors called. I don't know. I was too little to notice any of it. What followed were nine years of ping-pong existence, with my brother and I bouncing around between various relatives in Los Angeles, Stanton, El Monte, Buena Park, Corona, Hawaiian Gardens, Selma, and Fresno, California.

You might think that we would hate my mother for deserting us. I don't. My brother doesn't hold her responsible at all for what happened. No, recently I sat at her kitchen table and ate her homemade pumpkin cookies and held her hand and told her I love her. I really do. I told her how Ernie had said just that afternoon that he didn't blame her.

Nor do I.

She has suffered. She still bears some of the signs of a stroke. She and I do not talk about my seventeen years in prison nor my childhood of being dumped with various relatives or do-gooders when my dad just could not provide for us.

I do not recall him ever pleading with anybody to take us. He would just go visit somebody, then while we were playing, drive off. We might not see him again for months. Yet, ironically, he had a deep, fatherly affection for Ernie and me. We loved the rich sound of his booming laugh. We basked in his attention when he did come around.

Frequently, we ended up with my Aunt Margaret. Other times we stayed with my mother and her new husband, Frank Grijalva, and my half-sisters Lucy and Carmen and my half-brother, Ralph.

Ernie and I knew we were interlopers there. I remember Christmases when it seemed to Ernie and me that the other kids got a lot more presents. We deeply resented that, although my mother says today that we all got the same number of gifts. Nevertheless, that was when I first felt my pain, when I became a thief – around the age of nine.

I would visit my friends' homes and see their nice toys – and leave with their best stuff in my pockets. After a while, their mothers began to make the connection. "Don't invite Art over," they would warn their children. "He'll steal everything."

That hurt. I hated them for it.

Ernie and I learned to fight at an early age, using the many short-tempered adults around us as role models. Our lives were filled with anger, verbal disputes, physical aggression and mayhem.

The reason my father had quit working as an upholsterer was because of one of many fights with one of my uncles – right there in the house, in front of us kids. My uncle went after my dad with an axe. Defending himself, my father caught that axe in his right hand.

Blood went everywhere, but still he pounded my uncle into senselessness. Then they both went to the hospital. Since we didn't have the money for proper treatment, my dad came home with only a bandage.

His hand never was right again. Arthritis set in. He lost his livelihood – and had to work at shooting pool to make any real money.

Ernie and I observed these goings-on, learning the lesson that might makes right. We quickly learned to hit those who crossed us. A dog-eat-dog mentality prevailed. In order to survive, to protect ourselves, it was necessary to be ready to deal with challenges with our fists.

Even as very small children, Ernie and I tested one another and our cousins and the neighborhood kids and classmates, pushing and yelling and accusing and shoving. We were always ready to fight other kids. We were also good at getting them in trouble – and ourselves out of it, if possible – by manipulating the emotions of the adults in charge. We learned how to lie loudly and convincingly enough that justice could not prevail.

In return, we were readily picked on by the other children. But the lesson was that the child who was toughest prevailed. Usually that was Ernie and me – although we did not have any way of knowing the social toll it was taking on us. We grew increasingly incapable of functioning in civilized society.

Amid the hitting and lying and screaming and cursing, we grew streetwise. Disputes were resolved through abusive talk, aggression and outright violence. We saw what happens when one child succumbs to the greater physical and mental abilities of the other.

Power. Control.

We were alert and attentive witnesses to the verbal and physical fights of the violent adults around us. In almost every case the victor was the person who physically won the fight, and that person enjoyed the esteem and respect of onlookers. Such experiences reinforced the lessons that might, indeed, makes right, and that toughness is a virtue, while humility is not.

Today I can walk the streets of my disconnected childhood and look at the familiar smog-filtered sunlight, palm trees and pastel-colored stucco apartments.

My Aunt Margaret's neighborhood – where I stayed more than anywhere else – doesn't look like a ghetto. The gang writing on the cement walls calls out for street gang revenge for the drive-by killing of a teenage girl caught in recent deadly crossfire. One gang in a car opened fire on another gang on the sidewalk and the girl, a runaway phoning home to anxious parents, was killed.

As I stand on the elementary school playground where I smoked my first joint and went back to class high for the very first time, I understand why it is said that East L A neighborhoods are best understood with your eyes closed. Police and ambulance sirens, the insistent sputter of hovering police helicopters, blaring car alarms, the rapid pop-pop of distant gunfire – all blend together into an incessant, menacing background blur.

Here I first cringed under the disrespect of those who had everything I did not. But it was also here that I first felt the pain of first love.

She was my third-grade teacher.

CHAPTER THREE

A LITTLE BOY ABANDONED

I was eight years old.

Dad took Ernie and me to visit our Aunt Trina, one of Mom's sisters, who lived in El Monte, a small city in Southern California. She had always been very kind to us.

Then Dad had to run an errand. He didn't return for several years. He just left us there.

I remember waiting and waiting that first afternoon, hoping he would come back. I remember running to the window every time that a car went by, believing it was him. It was no secret that Aunt Trina was irritated that he had dumped us on her, again.

She had her own problems. She didn't need two little attention-demanding thieves and liars. We stayed maybe a day or so. Then my mother came over and got us.

My mom was very angry about it. She didn't have the time, space or energy for us in her life.

Because her new family's dining room table was just big enough for them, Ernie and I had to eat at a separate table away from my step-father Frank and my half-sisters, Lucy and Carmen, and my half-brother Ralph.

Ernie and I had to serve ourselves from the table, then be glared at if we came back for more.

It hurt to be segregated and treated as inferiors. It was hard to accept that our mom really didn't want us and that her husband could barely tolerate us.

Today, I have made my peace with both of them and am

welcome in their home. But it was hard when I was eight. They were a family. I was not part of it.

"You were a handful," Frank told me recently. "As a little boy, you were something else."

Well, I remember Ernie and me doing things to get their attention that must have been pretty irritating. In the Disney movie, Cinderella was kind and forgiving to her unloving step-family. She was selfless and sacrificial. She served their every need.

Not Ernie and me. We swiped their stuff.

We demanded their love and attention and if they wanted to treat us like brats, then we acted like brats. We made their lives miserable – and got a big kick out of it. You have to understand what is funny to an eight-year-old boy and his ten-year-old brother.

Giggling and whispering at night when everybody else is yelling at you that they are trying to go to sleep can be hilarious to two goofy little guys.

Driving a grown man to exasperation is very, very entertaining when you are eight. My stepfather, Frank, was easily goaded into fury.

If we could get the other kids into trouble, it was great, too – watching him beat them, particularly if they were innocent.

My brother had a wild sense of humor. He liked to trick people and do practical jokes. I always laughed when he made people scream and cuss. We were little urchins – alternately sullen, then suddenly rowdy and loud.

We began stealing from Mom's purse and from stores and getting into fights at school. That meant that Mom had to come down to the school and listen to the principal tell her how bad we were. It humiliated her. But at least it got her attention.

My favorite pastime was sneaking into the classroom at recess when no one was around and stealing candy and treats from the other kids' lunch boxes. I figured they were rich – at least compared to me – so they could afford it. On the rare occasions when I was caught, I was a master at lying my way out of it.

I could yell and carry on and hotly disavow all knowledge of the Twinkie I was still swallowing. I could accuse everybody else and totally confuse the issue by pointing fingers at other suspects and changing the subject and getting my accusers sidetracked.

One great way was to burst into tears and accuse White teachers of hating all Hispanic kids. They were stunned by my false accusation. Suddenly my sin was forgotten while they guiltily defended their lack of racial bias.

It was especially fun to get kids in trouble who had gotten me in trouble. I could lie to high heaven about whatever I chose and the teachers would believe me – while the falsely accused kid would weep and deny everything while I gloated and made faces – proud of my accomplishment.

I could bluff my way out of almost anything.

And I always took my revenge. I pounded people who tattled on me. I got them on the playground or after school on the way home. I could blacken eyes and bloody noses and hit kids so hard they could not breathe.

I would choke my opponent and pound their face into the dirt and take their lunch money and threaten that if they told anybody, I would get them much worse next time.

I could be their faithful friend, too. I could organize the playground. With my imagination, all the other boys were my motorcycle gang or my Mexican army. We would attack whoever I had picked to be the day's victim and make them plead for our mercy and give us all their candy or money or lunch tickets.

One time I stole five dollars from Mom's purse, and all that day at school I had lots of friends – you could buy a lot of candy for five dollars in the late 1950s! But when I got home there was a grim-looking Frank and a suspicious-looking Mom waiting for me. The friends who had come home with me rapidly disappeared from the scene. I was dragged into the house.

In our bedroom poor Ernie was already waiting, a sick look

on his face.

I denied any knowledge of the missing money, so Frank began to whip us with his belt. Ernie didn't confess because he was innocent and I was unwilling to admit to anything. So Frank just carried on whipping us.

I think I would have let him whip me all evening if it hadn't been for Ernie. He was getting it worse than me since he was older and they had decided he was the guilty one.

So, out of compassion for my brother, I owned up to the crime. Frank was so angry that he beat me until I could not walk. But somehow that beating was different from all the rest. I had a deep sense of satisfaction from knowing I had saved Ernie from any more suffering.

At elementary school I basked in my increasing reputation as a bad dude. I would challenge other kids and enjoy my power as they backed down and did whatever I demanded.

The meaner that kids thought I was, the nicer they all were toward me – even older ones. They didn't want any trouble. They thought I was crazy. They didn't want me getting them back – either pounding them physically or setting them up to get into big trouble for something they didn't do.

If you can believe this, sometimes I would even get paid to bully someone. I would just push the kid off his feet or knock his books out of his hands. But I had a tender heart. It rarely showed unless you noticed that I never attacked the weak or helpless – only the bullies, even if they were older than me!

I spent a lot of time at the principal's office.

I would carry on and deny all involvement in whatever I was accused of doing. He would sigh and shake his head. Because I could be so convincing, he had no idea what was the truth. I usually confused the issue so thoroughly that he just let me go.

I laughed all the way to class. This was fun. This was a great game – con the big man in charge.

More and more, however, Ernie and I were blamed for things we did not even do. We would protest and yell our innocence, but nobody knew what to believe. We were punished anyway – with the principal shrugging that even if we were innocent, this paddling was for all the things we had gotten away with.

That wasn't fair.

Mom and Frank usually just ignored the notes he sent home. When they talked to me about it, I would get sad and tell them that I was having a terrible time with my teachers. I was just too slow at school and the lessons were too hard for me, I would whimper, and that was why I was bullying the other kids.

That was ridiculous, of course. I was smarter than most. I just was having too much fun.

I have read that some psychologists believe that many little boys are potential criminals who find it perfectly natural to take things, break things, and beat people up. It's their parents' responsibility to work some of that out – to inhibit antisocial behavior, instill prosocial values, and cultivate the work ethic.

Well, that certainly described me. Only nobody paid enough attention to me to work anything out of me.

And I wasn't all that interested in cooperating with the program. Disrupting it was much more fun. Driving the teachers crazy was extremely entertaining. I was the sort of kid who put little mirrors on my tennis shoes, then stood in line behind girls in dresses, checking out the scenery until I got slapped in the face. Even at age eight, I thought it was worth it!

Then I was put into Miss Chenowith's third grade class. She was tall and pretty. She was in her early 20s and wore very stylish clothes. I liked her a lot.

After class one day she convinced me that if I worked hard, I could get 100 percent on the next spelling test. I believed her. I took the spelling books home and worked hard at it, remembering what she had told me. After the test I waited eagerly as she graded all the papers. There were only a few perfect scores, and mine was one of them!

To this day I am grateful to her, because her encouragement enabled me to teach myself to read later on when I was in prison. She was the only person who had ever believed in me, who ever told me that I had the potential to be someone. That made her my special friend.

But one day Miss Chenowith caught me rifling through her desk during recess.

"Arthur, what are you doing?" she demanded. I hated being called Arthur – I was Art.

She stood over me. In my hand was a roll of lunch tickets I had just taken from her desk. I flushed with shame. Usually I didn't mind being caught – since I made such a great game about lying my way out of it.

But this was different.

She was my special friend. I tried to run away, but she grabbed hold of my arm. I tried to hit out at her with my fists.

"Why are you doing this, Arthur?" she cried, holding on to me as I struggled. I began thrashing wildly and she kept telling me to calm down. Finally I bolted out of the classroom and made for the fence on the edge of the school.

I didn't think that any female, small or big, could outrun me, but she surprised me. She caught up with me before I could manage to get over the fence and pulled me off. I was so angry and embarrassed that I turned around to give her my best shot in the stomach. That one always worked on my half-sister Lucy!

But then I saw something which stopped me from hitting her – there were tears in her eyes. I could see that she felt for me. That broke my eight-year-old heart.

Her eyes were filled with tears of compassion for me. She really cared. I had never seen a grown-up cry before. I was angry about being caught, but her tears took all the fight out of me. I kept looking at her eyes as she slowly stood up and relaxed her grip on me.

Then I ran for it again!

But the principal grabbed me the next day and dragged me into his office.

"Blajos," he told me, "I've finally had enough of you and

your wild behavior. Attacking Miss Chenowith, one of our finest teachers, is the very last straw. I'm kicking you out of this school!"

I thought that if I was bigger, he wouldn't get away with talking to me like that. I hated my helplessness. I was angry that I wasn't big enough or strong enough to show him who was boss.

He picked up the telephone and called my mother and told her to come and pick me up.

She refused to come.

They argued for a while, then he slammed the phone down. He stared at me. Then, he gathered up my things and took me to the front door.

"You are expelled," he said. "Don't ever come back or I will call the juvenile authorities and you will be taken to jail for trespassing."

As I began the walk home alone, a car pulled up beside me. It was Miss Chenowith, offering me a ride home.

"No thanks," I yelled.

"Get in, Arthur," she insisted. "I want to talk to your mom. I want to tell her how well you've been doing in my class, and that you scored 100 percent in your spelling test."

But I didn't want her to meet my mom. I felt betrayed. Plus, I was embarrassed when my friends met my mother. I feared they could tell that she did not love me.

"Leave me alone," I screamed. "I don't go with strangers."

Finally she gave up and drove away.

I never saw her again.

CHAPTER FOUR

HARD STREET LESSONS

I was not permitted to return to school.

Although he hadn't done anything to Miss Chenowith, Ernie was expelled, too.

We were both written off as incorrigible delinquents. We didn't care. It meant that we could stay home and play all day, or so we thought.

Instead, it made Mom realize she just couldn't cope with us any more. She asked the county Social Services for help. It was decided that the best thing would be to send us to a boys' home in LaVerne, California.

That day a nice old lady came to our house and talked with Mom. Then Mom told us, "Ernie, Art, go and pack your things. You're going away with this lady to stay somewhere else – just for a little while. And the lady will buy you hamburgers on the way."

The promise of hamburgers persuaded us to co-operate! We jumped into the car with our few belongings, and the lady drove us to LaVerne, 45 miles away.

We were impressed by our first sight of the boys' home, which was a big granite mansion high in the Pomona foothills. It was a beautiful place, surrounded by 22 acres of land covered with eucalyptus trees and orange groves. But as we drove up the long driveway, I felt a sense of foreboding, as if something bad was going to happen to us there.

The nice old lady left us there in the care of a woman called Aunt Barbara and two big, strapping men known as Uncle John and Uncle Bill.

The boys' home was designed to accommodate boys who were troubled or orphaned. The place had been founded by a short, heavy-set man with a ruddy complexion. He had a real concern for boys in trouble and was always quick to lend them a helping hand.

He was fond of saying, "There ain't no totally bad boys." At that time, in 1959, the home housed about 100 boys aged between seven and eighteen.

All the staff members were addressed as "Uncle" or "Aunt".

Aunt Barbara would have the job of looking after us for the next three years. She was a Christian lady in her thirties who really cared about the little guys in her charge. When new boys arrived, she would talk with them and give them soft toys to help them settle in.

She gave me a stuffed lion, but I still wanted to run away. They gave us new clothes and shoes and then told us the rules. The older boys were housed in dormitories while the younger ones lived in cottages. This meant Ernie and I had to be separated at night, since he was old enough to go to the dorms.

I didn't like the idea at all of being separated from Ernie. He and I were used to watching each other's backs. We looked out for one another. I felt safe with him there. He was ten years old – worldly wise and mature in my eight-year-old eyes.

He was the only other person in the world who cared if I lived or died. I needed him. I played with him and constantly fought with him and made him mad at me lots of times. I could be a pest and embarrass him in front of his friends.

But I was his most faithful defender. I could turn into a crazed little wildcat if some kid was hurting him. If you fought one of us, you had to fight both of us.

Now for the first time since I was born, he and I had no choice about being separated.

We didn't like it.

Everything they did was different.

Every morning all the boys had to assemble around the flagpole and say the Pledge of Allegiance. In the evenings we stood and watched as the flag was lowered, and then we filed into the dining hall. Ernie and I had been used to Mom's little kitchen, so we felt uncomfortable and out of place among all these other boys.

At the first meal I jumped into my seat then awkwardly noticed that everybody else was standing. Aunt Barbara told me rather sternly that no one was allowed to sit down until grace had been said. This was a strange idea to me – praying before eating! I had never heard of thanking God for food. My family had never gone to any kind of church.

We prayed again at night – everybody reciting the Lord's Prayer beside their bed just before we were tucked in. I kind of liked it because it mentioned my name – "Art"!

But I grew weary of it. I would jump into bed quickly because I was sleepy, but Aunt Barbara would make me get up again and say the Lord's Prayer. I would then rattle it off, but she would stop me and make me say it properly.

I learned the prayer by heart, but I didn't feel any benefit from it.

On Sundays we had to go to a big church in Pomona. I hated it! I had to sing boring songs and listen to adults go on and on about things that I didn't understand.

Like most kids, I just tuned out the sermon. I might listen at the very first, but quickly it was over my head. I didn't know what any of it meant. I really didn't care, either. It had absolutely nothing to do with me.

Lots of the guys went down to the altar and became Christians. The adults prayed with them and declared how proud they were of them. Then the guys got dunked in the big baptistery behind the pulpit. I remember how it had this faded mural of a river flowing down through some fakey-looking trees.

I did not get dunked. I never made an altar call.

I watched, amazed, as a lot of the guys did. Afterward, they got to take communion too. I looked at the tiny little bit of cracker they got and the sip of grape juice and I didn't figure getting pushed underwater with all my good clothes on in front of everybody was worth it. Plus, I could tell that the adults really badly wanted me to do it. That was good enough reason to wait.

We did have some extremely happy times at the home at Christmas time.

The founder of the boys' home had some influential friends who used to invite us to parties at colleges and department stores and YMCAs. I loved getting Christmas presents. It was nice to have them given to me instead of having to steal them! I recall being taken to Disneyland by people from Cerritos College. Another Christmas we were taken to a party at a big Air Force base.

That was really exciting because they let us sit in the cockpit of one of their fighter planes. I also loved the carol singing. I remember one Christmas party when we were all in the dining hall in the home, there was a huge Christmas tree covered with pretty lights and presents. The grown-ups encouraged us to sing some Christmas songs and one of the boys sang *Silent Night* in German.

As he sang, I began to feel a strange sensation, of peace and well-being, as if some mighty warrior was smiling down on us and saying, "No harm can come to you. Everything is just fine."

I found this so moving that I wept. I was embarrassed, so I tried to hide behind the Christmas tree. A couple of grown-ups saw me and said, "Are you OK, son? Don't worry – it's all right to cry."

I didn't know what to say.

I just nodded, bowed my head and tried to be inconspicuous. I didn't know it at the time, but Ernie was also touched by that song and wept, too.

I didn't understand much about Christmas. Why would

people who didn't know us want to give us so much for nothing? I didn't worry about it. I took their neat things and looked forward to the next Christmas.

I made two friends: David, the tallest boy in my cottage, and little Robert, because he was different. He had a strange way of talking and was always getting into trouble, even fighting with the staff. But then they discovered that Robert was almost deaf, which explained most of his bad behavior.

People had thought he was a mean kid, but in fact he had just been frustrated because he couldn't hear properly. They got him a hearing aid, and that changed him dramatically. He started getting good grades in his schoolwork and didn't want to beat people up like he used to.

In fact, he rapidly turned into Aunt Barbara's favorite. He just wasn't much fun any more.

We spent most of our time at the home, but we also attended a public school.

There, David and I began to beat up the guys who weren't from the home because they thought they were better than us.

One day David and I tried to tattoo our names onto our fingers. The older boys had told us that if we cut the letters into our skin and then rubbed blue watercolor paint into the wounds, we would have tattoos.

All we got was into big trouble. The principal of the school called the boys' home and told them to come get us. Six-foot-tall Uncle John was so mad that he dragged David and me into the bathroom and rubbed off our "tattoos" with a scouring brush – that hurt!

Today you might say Ernie and I were strong-willed. Another term I have heard is "high-need". That was right. I needed somebody to care. I demanded it. And I absolutely refused to be ignored.

I was important; they would acknowledge that if it was the last thing I ever did. They would not make me shut up and sit down; they would recognize me.

Desperately I needed somebody to take me out of the nightmare of my life and force me to behave. I needed somebody to love me so totally and unconditionally that it would break my heart to disappoint them.

So why was my life so wrong? Why didn't anybody want me? I guessed it was because I was such a loser. I was mean and pushy and talked dirty if I felt like it. I stole things and lied to get myself out of trouble and made people cry. I had to force them to like me. To respect me.

Maybe they wouldn't love me, but at least they would be too scared to give me a hard time. They would acknowledge me.

And they'd have to let me say how things were going to be. I would have their respect – whether they gave it to me or if I had to force it from them against their will. They *would* respect me. They would not dare to hurt me. But I stayed afraid.

One night, I was awakened by loud whispering. I opened my eyes to see the boys who slept in my cottage holding hammers, picks and shovels, standing around me, saying, "Kill Art! Kill him! Kill him!"

In a panic, I dashed out into the cold, black night of the Pomona foothills.

I ran for my life. The other boys stayed in pursuit, gaining on me. The hill grew steeper. I gasped for air. I was scared and couldn't understand why they wanted to kill me. But they were relentless, and just kept shouting, "Kill Art!"

Just as I thought I was going to be killed – expecting hammers and shovels to come crashing down on me – something scared me even more – a deep growl from a nearby bush. The earth trembled.

Terrified, I spun to face my pursuers. But there was no one there, just deadly calm and cold blackness all around me. I heard the growl again. I ran back to the home. I picked up two big rocks, ready to strike anyone who tried to jump me.

In my room, everybody was in bed. Their shoes and pants were all neatly folded and put away. I put the rocks under my bed, just in case, and knocked on Aunt Barbara's door, waking her up.

She said it had been a nightmare and gave me a couple of aspirins. That next morning I had deep cuts and bruises on my feet and legs.

But the rocks weren't under my bed.

The nightmare began recurring. I would fall asleep, and it would start all over again. I would dream that I was awakened by the voices, and the whole frightening chase would start again — and I was powerless to stop it. Finally I was taken to the doctor, who gave me some pills to help me to sleep. After about a week the dream faded away, but I remembered those voices and the strange growl from the bush for a long time afterwards.

What did it mean?

What was I running from?

Was I being warned that something else awaited? I didn't know. But thinking about it made me shiver.

I was only nine.

CHAPTER FIVE

THE AMAZING McKENZIE BROTHERS

About that time, Ernie and I discovered that we were athletes. We could run.

In a track meet at the boys' home, I took first place in the 50-yard dash. Ernie came first in the 100-yard dash and also excelled at the high jump. We were delighted about this and lapped up the attention we received and the handshakes and congratulations.

It was cool. It was great.

A while back, I was reading a *Sports Illustrated* magazine. An article told about a teacher at the high school in Boyle Heights, one of the many places that Ernie and I had lived with relatives.

Boyle Heights is surrounded by neighborhoods that are wracked frequently by the noise of gang gunfire. This teacher was used to it – and taught only students with serious discipline problems: "hard-core truants," according to the article, "the terminally bored, those who do more than dabble in drugs and alcohol, gang members and other troublemakers who don't belong in regular classrooms."

"The kids who end up here," the Boyle Heights principal told *Sports Illustrated,* "are the terrors of their schools."

Well, that was Ernie and me.

One time my brother and I took part in a physical fitness competition. Before he quit, Ernie did 1,000 sit-ups! That was a tremendous feat even for an adult. I remember being greatly impressed by the respect Ernie gained from grown men and the tougher boys.

Ernie paid a price for the glory he won: he ended up with two huge, bleeding blisters on his buttocks! He could barely walk for days.

But it was worth it. The lesson our winning taught us was that we could win respect through physical toughness. So, we applied ourselves with a passion. We entered every competition we could.

Our reputation as athletes grew as we brought back ribbons and medals and trophies. Our sporting talents even enabled us to evade punishment, since if we were being disciplined, we would miss upcoming competitions, and that would be bad for the home.

I loved being the hero. There was no thrill in defeat and I didn't particularly gain any release from competition. I just loved being the big star in the limelight when I won. So, I was ripe for disaster. Ernie was, too.

Just as our egos were swelling, two extremely athletic brothers named Bernard and Charlie Mitchell came to the home. They loved running just for running's sake. Plus, they were faster than either Ernie or me.

Uncle John immediately put them on the track team. The first time out, Charlie beat me in my best event – the 50-yard dash. Meanwhile, Bernard went off and left Ernie in his event, the 100-yard dash.

All of a sudden we Blajos brothers were has-beens at ages nine and eleven. We were dethroned champions. The respect and attention that had been lavished on us abruptly belonged to the Mitchell brothers.

We were devastated.

So, we plotted our return. Rather than training and getting into better shape than the Mitchells, Ernie and I decided to jump them. We figured after we had blackened their eyes and knocked out a few teeth, they would think twice about making us look bad.

So I cornered nine-year-old Charlie and goaded him into a

fight. To my astonishment he was eager and ready to mix it up with me. Furthermore, he was a much better fighter than me. After he hit me pretty solidly several times, I grabbed a tree limb and beaned him from behind with it, making his scalp bleed. He ran off crying.

I was thrilled with his cowardice. In my eyes, I had won.

Meanwhile, Ernie challenged Bernard, who quickly got the upper hand while a crowd of home kids cheered. I was so angry over their disloyalty that I picked up a rock to smash Bernard's head. Suddenly the air was pierced by his loud scream. Ernie had his ear clenched between his teeth and was close to ripping it right off! Just in the nick of time, a staff member arrived and yanked Ernie off him.

But, still, Bernard's ear required several stitches. And we remained dethroned as the home's champions. Bernard and Charlie were the new heroes on the track field.

It was devastating. Ernie and I went from heroes to curs. We sulked around in our disgrace. If we had enjoyed running, losing would not have had nearly the sting. However, we only liked the fame and glory.

Then the Mitchells got theirs. Two new idols arrived, the amazing McKenzie brothers.

They were the first *cholos* or Hispanic gang members I ever encountered. They both had tattoos that said *La vida loca* – "the crazy life."

They knew how to kick-box.

They talked like *cholos*, using profane Spanish street slang, which shocked and impressed me immensely. I mimicked their every word – particularly the dirty phrases. With them, in either English or Spanish, ordinarily clean words took on filthy, sniggering meanings.

But even their clean conversation was colorful. "Hina" meant girlfriend. "Placa" was the police. A "rata" was an informer. "Cha-cha" meant homosexual; "cuete" was gun; "fiero" knife; "vato firme" a dependable guy. They greeted everybody,

"¡Orale, ese!" or "¿Eh, carnalito, qué hay de nuevo?" Like all slang, it was gibberish except to insiders. Literally those two phrases mean, "Say it, man," and "Hey, little brother, what is new?" However, either one makes just as much sense as the English slang equivalent: "What's up, dude?"

From the McKenzie brothers, we all learned how to cuss proficiently – both in English and Spanish.

Actually, they weren't real *cholos*. Chuck was sixteen years old and blond. Dennis was fourteen and had freckles. Sons of a white, drug-addicted prostitute, they had been taken in off the street by a Hispanic family. Living in the barrio, the angry boys had taken on the *movidas* of street-gang thugs – the moves and the attitude.

Alarmed and worried about the safety of their own children, their foster parents reluctantly placed them in the boys' home.

The McKenzie brothers would stand with their chins out in defiance, their feet pointing east and west, their hair slicked back. They had the *cholo* clothing style down to perfection – shiny, black, pointy French-toed shoes, high-waisted khaki pants starched with a razor-sharp crease all the way up to the waist, and tucked-in t-shirts under long-sleeved, Pendleton-type shirts worn with the tails out and only the top two buttons buttoned.

For years to come, this would be the standard dress code in some parts of California, especially among Hispanic kids. You had to dress this way – or your local variation of it – if you wanted to be known as a tough guy.

And I did.

At age nine, I could be a *cholo* without having to win stupid track meets.

The McKenzie brothers had a deep and bitter anger against all authority. Quietly and behind the backs of the home's staff, they retaught us lessons that we had already learned, but seemed newly exciting and important at the time – such as you must win every fight, whatever it takes. If you lose, you will be rejected by your friends.

Well, I had already seen that.

And I didn't like being rejected. I had already experienced so much of that. My mother had abandoned me as a baby. Repeatedly, my dad had dumped me at relatives' homes. All too often, they did a fancy quickstep – pawning us off on somebody else before we settled in.

I had failed at school – both scholastically and socially. I had failed Miss Chenowith. Now I had lost all my respect at a boys' home full of disloyal losers.

All my life, I had been bounced from one temporary home to another, made to feel like a second-class human being no matter how hard I tried.

The McKenzie brothers pointed a way out. I hated being a disrespected little kid. I wanted to be a feared man. I could be that as a *vato loco* and a *cholo*. Nobody would dare to reject me – even if I was still a soprano seven years away from needing to shave.

Being exactly like the McKenzie brothers, feared and respected and reluctantly accepted by everyone, became my conscious goal. I wanted people to be cautious and unsure around me. I wanted them to be wary and off balance.

The McKenzie brothers made no effort to talk like everybody else, either. Instead, they spoke with an exaggerated Hispanic accent. The way they spoke English was with an exciting, cool hyped-up Spanish pronunciation. It worked. It set people back. They were off-balance. You could see the fear in their eyes. It was great.

I learned from the McKenzie brothers how important it was to guard my personal image, too. Physical appearance – clothes and grooming – were vital. They always looked sharp.

The McKenzie brothers showed Ernie and me how important image and *movidas* – "moves" – are in how a person is viewed by those around him. To be respected, it is important to have the right look.

Also, if we lost a fight, it was important, not only in the eyes of our opponent, but also in the eyes of everyone who saw what had happened, to avenge ourselves dramatically, quickly and violently.

To maintain our honor Ernie and I had to demonstrate that we were not to be messed with. The McKenzie brothers showed us that in order to accomplish that, we would have to stick together. We already knew that – but this just verified everything. If an enemy beat up one of us, we and our friends would have to ambush him when he was off by himself. He would have to pay the price. He had to see that taking on the Blajos brothers was dangerous. It could get him killed. It would always spark revenge.

But this is the stuff that spawns blood feuds. Soon your enemy walks around only with his friends, constantly stalking you – just as you are stalking him.

Over the years it has disintegrated into the very thing that curses the streets of America's inner cities today – ongoing vengeance without end. Nobody remembers its beginnings, either. But the blood continues to flow.

Maybe it is hard for people out in the safe suburbs to understand. In polite, middle-class society, people are not obliged to retaliate physically after they have been degraded or taken advantage of.

They may feel a great need to defend themselves during a robbery or a mugging, or to behave in such a way so as to deter aggression – such as staying behind locked doors with their car windows rolled up.

But the middle class who make up most of America's population are much more likely than the street-wise to walk away from a fight with their self-esteem intact – and may even have the wisdom to flee without any worry that their self-respect or esteem might be diminished.

More than anything, the McKenzie brothers taught that blood must flow. If we were jumped and beaten up, seeking revenge was mandatory. It might mean going to get a weapon and blasting an enemy — or their relatives — into eternity.

But the message had to be clear: *leave the Blajos brothers alone.*

Identity, self-respect and honor were intricately tied up with the way that the McKenzie brothers viewed the world threatening us all. Middle class kids had other ways of gaining status and regard. They were not dependent on such physical displays.

We had no other way.

Nobody had ever showed us how to lose gracefully at a track meet. Nobody had talked with us about the honor of mere competition. When we lost, we lost everything.

The McKenzie brothers showed us that one of the best ways to demand respect was to demonstrate fearlessness. That was shown by stealing richer people's good stuff, messing with an adversary's woman, throwing the first punch against somebody bigger, getting in someone's face even though you knew they carried a knife, or defying authority, such as a teacher or the principal or your cottage "aunt" in a way that everybody saw you momentarily in charge, holding the upper hand — making them look like a fool.

You had to show a total lack of fear in the face of death. To risk dying to preserve your image was completely cool. In fact, the clear risk of violent death was definitely preferable to being humiliated or disrespected, particularly by strangers. Ernie and I yearned for people to whisper in awe: "Those Blajos brothers are the baddest dudes on the street."

Of course, such fearlessness has dangerous implications for the future of civilization. The McKenzie brothers taught Ernie and me that the system had already lost its threat over us.

Society threatened us with punishment.

We laughed at it.

The police threatened us with prison.

We sneered and announced that we looked forward to going.

The system threatened us with violent death. We bragged that we were ready to go out in a blaze of glory.

The system had done nothing for us and now the McKenzie brothers demonstrated it could do nothing to us. *People feared them.* People looked at them in alarm – and gave them a wide berth.

I desperately wanted that.

What the McKenzie brothers offered me was not social acceptance or popularity. Both were far beyond my grasp anyway. The McKenzie brothers' *macho*, tough-guy alternative was extremely attractive to a little fighter on the doorstep of adolescence.

It's a mystery to me how those McKenzie brothers ended up at the boys' home. They weren't really the home's usual material at all. They only stayed a few months – but long enough to change my life forever. They were caught with switchblades, which they refused to hand over, so they were sent off to the city's Juvenile Hall. Chuck McKenzie was destined to die of a drug overdose, and Dennis McKenzie has spent most of his adult life in prison. They were my heroes and my mentors.

Even after they were gone, although I was painfully aware of my physical weakness and smallness, I was determined to be a winner – like them – rather than a victim.

Ernie was going through the same thing – only as an eleven-year-old. He was beginning to get his growth and starting to show muscles. But we were both just as mean as the other – and we stuck together no matter what. We became known as "the fighting Blajos brothers."

We strutted and sneered and glowered like the McKenzie brothers. We ironed our pants with perfect creases and greased our hair back. We grew more violent and dangerous. The staff at the boys' home had an increasingly difficult time coping with us.

Ernie and I had learned we could not survive if we were not sufficiently aggressive. If one of us lost a fight on the playground, the other would say, "We got to pay them back, *ese*."

If someone picked on us, you had to straighten them out. We

quit crying. Our tears dried up. We learned that tears solved nothing. Instead, if somebody hurt you up in any way, you got back out there and messed him up – and good. You hurt him in a way that he would never make that mistake again.

On one occasion I was swearing colorfully at Aunt Barbara and Tony, one of the tough, older boys, walked past me and said, "Keep it up, dude, and some day you'll be in Dorm 1."

That was the dorm for the oldest and toughest boys in the home.

That was an exciting idea to me!

Maybe some day I would be just like Tony! He had tattoos, he shaved, he wore a black leather jacket and Levis – a sort of James Dean "Rebel Without a Cause" look. But he did not become my idol – since he was not a *cholo*, a Hispanic.

During those final years at the boys' home, Ernie and I must have received every form of punishment the staff knew – and I think they invented a few more just for us!

We were made to sweep the home's long driveway. We endured the "cubby hole," which was a very small room with no bed or lights. We had slaps on the face, our heads knocked together, our mouths washed out with soap – and we were made to hold heavy rocks with our arms outstretched.

They really did their best to discipline us. They cared about us. But we were determined to be *cholos*.

We were on the road to destruction, and we were about to shift into high gear.

CHAPTER SIX

I BECOME CHIEF OF THE SINNERS

About the time I turned eleven, the boys' home staff had finally had enough of Ernie and me. They located our Dad and gave him an ultimatum: *Come and get your sons or else we will hand them over to the state.*

The state would have sent us to the Juvenile Hall in Los Angeles. Dad didn't want that, so he came and took us away with him. He didn't have anywhere for us to live, so he took us to our Aunt Dorothy and Uncle Jim's home in Norwalk, California.

We stayed there for a few months. They had eight children of their own, so they didn't welcome us with much enthusiasm.

Ernie was now in junior high school. I was still a grade schooler – in the sixth grade.

Uncle Jim's family believed in hard work. They would drive up and down the state during the grape season, working in various places. Sometimes we went with them.

The work was easy for us since Ernie and I were so physically fit. The little money we earned went to our father.

Sometimes Dad, Ernie and I would collect cow manure from the local dairy farms and take it in a truck to the nearby avocado and citrus groves. It was hard, dirty, smelly work, but I enjoyed it – particularly since I got to be with my dad.

I didn't know it, but I needed my dad.

I believe he enjoyed my company, too.

Everything might have been OK if I hadn't had to go to school.

The area of Norwalk where Aunt Dorothy and Uncle Jim lived was a Hispanic barrio known as Carmelas. However, we were sent to a public grade school where most of the pupils were English-speaking and middle class. It was there that I experienced my first real taste of racism. Up to this time I hadn't realized that people could hate me just because I was Hispanic.

I thought being a *vato loco* was cool.

I had no idea that people would hate me for it.

Of course, I really didn't help things with my cocky attitude. I defied the Anglos who were my age to reject me. I played being a *cholo* and a *vato loco* to the hilt. So they did reject me.

On my first day at this new school, I quickly got the message: I was poor, I was behind academically, and I was the wrong race. The teacher asked one of the kids, a blond boy named Mark, to show me around the school grounds.

"Do I have to?" he whined.

Then she asked somebody else, who refused, and then someone else whined his way out of it, too.

Nobody wanted to help me out. Standing there in the front of the room with nobody wanting to assist me, I began to feel extremely self-conscious. I realized that purely because I was Hispanic and poor, they didn't like me.

I didn't know how to deal with this situation. I had never been treated this way before.

By this stage of my life it had almost become an instinct to use violence to make an impression. I knew it took courage to take someone on and beat them and so win respect. My pride fueled that courage as I went up to Larry, the biggest kid in the class, and started talking to him. I wanted to make my presence known. I refused to accept his snub.

But Larry and the other kids made it clear that I was an outsider, someone they didn't want around.

I knew it was time to do something about this before it was too late. So I started hitting Larry.

He was the biggest kid in the class, but I took him on and

won, and it bought me respect. I also chased Mark all over the school for refusing to show me around.

Within weeks, we wore out our welcome with Aunt Dorothy and Uncle Jim, so we moved into the home of my Aunt Margaret at Boyle Heights in East Los Angeles. She was a stunning beauty with red hair and green eyes. Ernie and I had always been fond of her because she was kind to us. She was comparatively well off and a soft touch!

The neighborhood consisted of Hispanics, Italians and Jews.

One of our Italian neighbors, Ol' Papa Joe, was always screaming at us not to touch his "machine" – his car. His wife used to invite us in to eat some of her fresh pastries, and Papa Joe would give us a sip of his homemade wine.

It made my head spin and my chest burn. I liked the sensation and wanted more. I wanted to get drunk like the older guys – and be crazy like them, staggering around, saying anything I pleased.

Sometimes Ernie and I would pretend to be drunk – playing out in the yard like we were too plastered to stand or talk right. It was fun. But we wanted the real thing. We had a Jewish friend named Sonny. His mom was always embarrassing him by bringing food out to him when we were playing baseball in the street. Before he was allowed to play, he had to finish all his homework. Today he is probably a lawyer or a doctor!

My aunt would ask if I had any homework. Truthfully, I would answer that I didn't – I'd thrown it away.

After one semester at Evergreen Elementary School, I moved on to Hollenbeck Junior High where Ernie was already attending. It was there that I became the leader of my own gang – by accident. Standing in the lunch line in school, a kid told me to give him 25 cents because he didn't have enough money. I didn't like his arrogant tone, so I refused.

He seemed surprised.

"Don't you know who I am?" he asked.

"I don't care who you are!" I stated flatly.

"I'm Richard Vargas, the leader of the Sinners!" he told me as if I ought to be impressed. Standing with him were some of his gang members and a couple of girls.

My pride flared up. "I don't care who you are!" I shouted.

"Do you want to get down?" he demanded in Spanish. This was an open challenge to fight. I accepted casually in my very best and most profane *cholo* talk, learned from the McKenzie brothers.

Everybody whispered in awe.

At that school all fights were fought in one of two designated places.

If it had been after school we would fought on Blueberry Hill where everyone could watch. If you were going to fight there, you had better win – because everybody would see!

But as this was during school hours, I followed Richard to the back of the buildings. I felt confident that I would be able to handle myself pretty well against him.

What I didn't expect was an ambush! About six of his friends leaped out on me and beat me up, leaving me bleeding on the ground. They never gave me a chance.

It was the lunch hour, so I had time to go to the bathroom and wash the blood off my face before going back to class.

But I was seething with anger, thinking about how I was going to pay Richard back for what he had done to me. He had humiliated me and I had to get even. It was a matter of honor.

A couple of hours later I saw Richard standing with some of his gang. My new friend Joe Cortes was with me. The moment I saw Richard I put down my books, took off my shirt and handed it to Joe.

My eyes were fixed on him.

I couldn't hear or see anything else.

Everybody quit talking. They stared at me in absolute awe. I had good muscles for a little seventh grader. Plus, it was extremely dramatic to peel off your shirt like that. It meant you were serious about making blood flow.

As I walked up to him, I turned into a crazed windmill. I started punching and kicking him. He went down and I was all over him. I kicked him in the privates, I slammed him in the ribs. I pounded his face and his nose until blood was everywhere.

It took two male gym teachers to drag me off him. When I came to my senses I looked down and saw a bloody mess on the floor – it was Richard. He was crying and writhing in pain.

I was suspended from school for a week and Richard had to spend a couple of days in the hospital. When I came back I saw him still with bandages on standing in the corridor.

His gang walked towards me. He glared behind them. I thought they were going to jump me again and take revenge. So I got ready for them.

But to my surprise they told me that because I had downed Richard, I was the new leader of the Sinners. The survival of the fittest was their rule. I had gained their respect.

That was a pivotal point in my life. It reinforced my belief that "might is right." I had become a "homeboy." I was a real gang member – not a little kid just wishing and trying to look the part.

As the new leader of the Sinners I had the respect, acceptance and security I had always wanted. That gang became my whole life. Its members were my family. None of us were older than twelve. But we were ready to take on East Los Angeles. The Sinners went on to become part of the First Flats gang, one of the most notorious groups in the barrio.

Meanwhile Ernie's life was developing along similar lines to mine. We were by now fighting a lot with Dad, who had rented the house across from my aunt. Ernie and I lived in both places. On one occasion I threatened him and was rewarded with a straight right hook that sent me to the floor! Our family had not been together more than a few months and it was already coming apart at the seams.

Ernie and I started smoking cigarettes. Dad knew we smoked,

but we took care not to do it in front of him. We were also smoking marijuana. I started experimenting with amphetamine pills, which we called "fender benders."

Girls were beginning to play an important part in my life, too. Adolescence was upon me like a fever. That was why I befriended Joe Cortes — he had two beautiful sisters named Vicky and Pat. At every opportunity I would walk home with Joe after school just to be with his sisters.

They were both gang girls with short, tight skirts and beehive hairdos. I was never a smooth-talking conversationalist with girls, but I knew what was easy on my eyes! At one point I had a nice girlfriend called Jenny, whose name I tattooed onto my hand. I later burned it off with a cigarette after we had a fight.

But what mattered to me most of all was my reputation in the neighborhood and what my brothers in the gang thought of me. I didn't want to get good grades at school, I didn't want to become a dentist or a scientist or a carpenter or a plumber. I just wanted to have fun right then and there as a good gang member, a solid homeboy.

I never really made a conscious decision to get into the gang culture. It just seemed the natural thing to do. I never had any awareness that what I was doing was wrong or that I could choose to do something else.

The only effective influences in my life had been Miss Chenowith and Aunt Barbara, but their input was minimal compared to the gang culture and the powerful peer pressure which it involved. My only reality was the one I lived with at school and on the streets, all day, every day.

Gang life formed a huge underground subculture. We were well into the 1960s and California was rocking with the rebellion against authority that would sweep across America during the Vietnam war and the flower-power era. Suddenly, it was cool to be part of an ethnic minority struggling against poverty and prejudice and injustice. The American Civil Liberties Union was rushing into place court decisions that were tying the hands of civil authorities.

After John F. Kennedy's assassination, President Johnson's "Great Society" and his War on Poverty poured hundreds of thousands of dollars into the hands of anybody who could claim to help the disadvantaged or oppressed. The new media gloried in it – heaping guilt on middle-class America for everything that was wrong in society.

The African-Americans – whom we called *mayates* – had Malcolm X and Martin Luther King. We had Che Guevera making revolution in Bolivia and Cesar Chavez boycotting the grapes in northern California. They had Black Power. We had the La Raza movement – with people talking about Chicano pride and the revival of the ancient Aztec religion, and Mexico taking back California and Arizona and Texas since they supposedly had been annexed illegally by the United States.

It was just so much talk to us kids on the street. We were more interested in getting high. We were into sniffing glue and other solvents and into smoking marijuana.

As we got older, we became increasingly violent. Money and girls became more important to me. I was committing robberies and other crimes so I could have a good time.

I was graduating to the big time.

CHAPTER SEVEN

A BUNCH OF LITTLE ROOSTERS

One evening when I was 14 years old, I was walking along the street, high on glue and barbiturate pills. It was an explosive combination, a cocktail which loosened my inhibitions and brought out my aggressions. I noticed there was a car cruising along behind me with its headlights off.

Someone got out, came up behind and grabbed my shoulder. I assumed it was a rival gang member, so I spun round and hit him squarely in the jaw with my fist. It was a lucky punch and he fell to the ground. Because of the drugs, my inhibitions were down and I went crazy, kicking him again and again where he lay.

But, in fact, he was not a gang member but a narcotics police officer. His partner ran over and clubbed me repeatedly over the head with his flashlight. They eventually got me into handcuffs and one of them beat me up in the back of the car all the way to Hollenbeck Police Station.

By the time we got there I had bruises all over my body, blood in my hair and plenty of bumps on my skull. The station commander had huge hands and wore black gloves. I imagined that he was going to pound me with his fists, but instead, he was angry with his two officers for over-reacting and beating me up so badly. Because I was tall for my age the LA police thought I was an adult suspect they had been looking for on the streets.

The cuffs were taken off me and I was put in a holding room. Soon Dad came. There was an expression of agony on his face as I told him what had happened. In his way, he really did care about me. They booked me for assault but, to my surprise, they then let me go home with Dad.

I was given a suspended sentence, but it was revoked two weeks later after I became involved in a fight at school. Instead of going to "Juvie" – Los Angeles Juvenile Hall, I was sentenced to a California Youth Authority camp.

The minute I walked into the yard, I was greeted in exaggerated, *vato loco*-style Spanish by a dude from school named Puppet, who I knew had been in trouble with the law since age ten for truancy and writing graffiti. He wasn't in the Sinners, but he had been a gang member since age nine. He was awaiting trial for armed robbery. He and a 23-year-old cousin had gotten high and knocked over a convenience grocery. They had been so stoned that they stopped just outside the door and used the coins they'd taken from the cash register to play pinball.

Standing beside him was a big guy called Oso, in for violating a court-imposed curfew imposed for hitting his abusive father and sending him to the hospital. Oso had told the judge he was sick and tired of being told what to do – resulting in a quick, three-year sentence.

There were a lot of gang members at the camp – many from rival street gangs. However, Puppet quickly explained to me that the old hostilities from our neighborhoods did not matter. Instead, the bad blood was mostly racial. Hispanics stuck together against the Whites and the Blacks – who also hated each other.

Puppet took me to meet the leader of the Hispanics, who was named Luís.

He looked me over in silence. He did not say anything. He was watching my moves. I waited, being careful not to show him anything that would make him think I was weak.

"You are *mero-mero* of the Sinners," he said in an exaggerated Spanish accent that I had not heard since the McKenzie brothers had been kicked out of the boys' home.

I nodded. *Mero-mero* was an enormous compliment. It means

something like "best of the best."

"That *cliqua*, it is bad," he said, his voice respectful, acknowledging that I had led a mean bunch of guys. "Hey, *ese*," he said, glancing away. "At age fourteen beating up a police officer makes you nearly legendary. We won't tell nobody you were high and done it by accident."

He smiled.

I had to laugh.

He was cool. I liked him immediately. He was no ordinary criminal.

That night, I got a bunk right in the middle of the Hispanic guys. We all slept in an open dormitory. Probably around 2 am, I woke up, startled. Puppet had his hand on my mouth. He pointed.

Across the room, there was a struggle. I pulled myself up on my elbow. In the darkness, I watched two Black kids silently rape a White boy right there in the open dorm with nobody doing anything about it. The Blacks were both about fifteen. The White boy was maybe thirteen, but seemed even younger.

Nobody did anything. Puppet looked at me and rolled his eyes. I tried not to show how terrified I was. Lots of people were awake – but a lot of them acted like they were sleeping or just didn't care – as if that sort of thing happened regularly.

The lesson was clear to me. The White kid had nobody to protect him.

That little White boy meant nothing to anybody. Even the tough White kids didn't want him.

After the assault was over, the thirteen-year-old curled up on the floor, crying. He whimpered that he wanted to go home. He called for his mother. Everybody ignored him. They acted as if nothing had happened. No staff came. No guards.

I turned my face away.

I vowed silently that I would not be a victim here. He was weak. He was helpless. He cried. He did not fight back. And nobody came to his defense. That night, he huddled on the floor, leaning against his bed, crying that all that he wanted was to go home – that he missed his mother.

The next morning, he chewed up some pieces of a broken light bulb – trying to kill himself. That landed him in five days of detention.

That was where they found him Friday afternoon, hanged in front of his bunk, a bed sheet tied around his neck. A guard rushed in, lifting him to relieve the weight on his neck. But he had no pulse. He was dead.

I remember seeing the body. No crude tattoos adorned his neck, chest or arms like they did most of the other kids. He left behind a note. The counselor made up copies and put them everywhere.

The kid's mother came to the front gate and picked up the body with the coroner. She screamed and wept.

We watched. Nobody said anything.

Luís was very cool. In the yard and in class, he carried himself as if he didn't have a care in the world. What Oso told me about him blew me away. Luís had been a straight-A student in East Los Angeles. Early one Saturday, his mother made him go buy groceries. He didn't want to. He liked reading and lifting weights with his mom's boyfriend. An aspiring artist, Luís often sat in his bedroom sketching. For company, he had only one friend, another boy who hated school because he was always picked on, too.

Both boys were being targeted by a particular gang because they would not join. It got so bad that Luís rarely left the apartment. Often, alone, he would stand at his fourth-floor bedroom window overlooking the playground of their housing project and watch the other children play.

But one Saturday, his mother gave him $10 for groceries and Luís headed down the sidewalk. Quickly, he was surrounded by about ten of the Hoyo Mara gang boys. They taunted him and one of them grabbed his $10.

Angry, Luís began to back up the walk when a thirteen-year-old named Huero came from behind and slammed his legs out from under him, making Luís, who was big for his age, crash forward to the ground, injuring his hand.

The gang members started kicking him as he floundered on the ground. He was scared and convinced they were going to kill him. Dodging their kicks, he had a strange vision of his mother crying because he was dead.

He looked up to see a sixteen-year-old named Tuffy coming at him with a knife. What happened next Luís remembers only as a blur. He wrestled with Tuffy. Then the older boy lay motionless on the ground. He had been stabbed three times in the chest.

"Leave me alone! Leave me alone!" Luís was heard shouting as he ran, holding the knife, which he told his mother he grabbed when Tuffy dropped it.

As Luís ran away, he dropped the knife on a stairway, and police never found it. Teary-eyed and bloody, with a swollen hand, he ran to his mother in the kitchen.

"He just stood there crying," she told the judge. "He wouldn't move. I kept asking, 'What happened?' He said, 'I didn't mean to hurt anybody.'"

Luís was charged as a juvenile and sent to the camp. Because the other boy was dead, Luís was sentenced to stay until he was an adult. Somehow, nobody cared that he had been an honor student or had stayed out of the gangs or that it was self-defense.

I felt enormous respect for him. He was a victim, but he had turned it around. He was the leader of the White Fence gang who were constantly at war with other neighborhoods.

And he had gotten tough when he had to.

The gang culture was more powerful inside the camp than it was on the streets. The major recreation at the camp was fighting with members of rival gangs. As I think back now, I realize that everybody enjoyed it.

It was rare for anybody to get killed. We were just a bunch of little roosters strutting around challenging each other. We

Hispanic dudes got off on loyalty. We were family – no matter what gang we'd hung with outside. Inside, we were brothers through *la raza* – our race. We were each other's protectors.

But nothing was absolutely certain – ever.

"*Cuidate,*" said Oso one day, glancing at Puppet, who was shooting baskets. Another guy, Donald, nodded at me darkly. "Be careful."

It was a warning – of what I was not certain. I did not know Puppet had a history of tremendous emotional problems. Supposedly his camp record showed twenty separate disciplinary problems since the beginning of the year: lateness, refusing to work, cutting class, insubordination, refusing to stand for the Pledge of Allegiance, chasing another student out of the dining hall, disrupting a work party, gang writing and tattooing.

Then, one day, there was an argument with a staff counselor. Puppet stormed out of the office without permission.

He went to his dorm, got a homemade knife, then went back to the counselor's office. He walked in, stabbed the staffer multiple times in the neck and shoulder, then walked out.

Puppet then went to class – but with blood all over his trousers. He had lost his mind. If you are going to kill somebody, you don't walk around with their blood on your clothes.

Plus, the counselor was only injured.

Puppet told the judge that he was sick of being told what to do by the camp officials, the guards, the counselor, his parents – that he wanted to be free. He also said that he had thought seriously about killing Luís and me.

We never saw him again. I do not know what happened to him.

CHAPTER EIGHT

PRELUDE TO PRISON

After six months at the Muntz Youth Authority Junior Camp, I ran away.

When they caught me I was sent to the Youth Authority jail at Paso Robles in Central California.

During my eight months there in 1965 I learned the *movidas* or "moves." I knew what they were from the McKenzie brothers and from camp. I had mimicked the gestures, the way to stand and the general attitude.

However, this time, it was serious. These were strict rules of conduct which each race had to abide by. The Hispanics' *movidas* were: don't eat with Blacks, Whites or Asians; always dust off your rear trousers pockets before sitting down; always dress smartly, with shiny shoes and creased pants. You were representing your race.

Never, ever could you back out of a fight.

My friends and I were now turning into young men. Macho mustaches were sprouting on our upper lips and we had a lot of tattoos. These served as identity cards, establishing our gang allegiance. They were a declaration of faith and loyalty. They showed that we belonged to a family.

Our violence became more mature and dangerous. Kids from different races who had once been my friends were now my sworn enemies. Also, some people who were inseparable drifted apart.

Ernie and I saw less and less of each other. We went our own way. Mostly my friends were people with whom I spent time in jail.

An Orange County, California, study shows 70 percent of all juveniles who've had one arrest are never arrested again. Another 20 percent commit two or three subsequent crimes, but then give up their criminal ways and do not get re-arrested.

This means that up to 80 percent to 90 percent of all kids who are arrested and must appear in court say to themselves, "Whoa, I'm not going to go through that again," according to Tom Higgins, head of the District Attorney's juvenile division for the southern part of Los Angeles County. "Not because they got any kind of rehabilitation from the court, but because the experience was life-changing for them."

On the other hand, about 8 percent to 10 percent of kids seem to be unreachable – once they've embarked upon serious crime. *That was me.*

"I deeply feel that there are very few twelve- or fourteen-year-olds who are unsalvageable," said Clyde Crohnkhite, former police chief of Santa Ana and ex-deputy chief of the Los Angeles Police Department. "I have found again and again that adults who commit serious, habitual, violent crimes cannot be changed easily if at all. But young people, in varying degrees, can definitely be changed. They are in a learning mode."

Unless they are sociopaths, Crohnkhite said, youngsters have the ability to rearrange their priorities and goals. "Sociopaths – which constitute less than one percent of the popuation – don't feel remorse, aren't concerned if they hurt others and live only for today."

You know, I believe America was at a crossroads in those days.

I did not know it. At age fourteen, I had no idea I was growing up in a transition generation. I was having too exciting a time being a *vato loco* and hanging out with my friends. But I am a Baby Boomer.

Boomers have been in more trouble with the authorities than any generation before us. As we Baby Boomers came of "crime age," crime rates soared. In 1960, only 1,887 crimes were committed for every 100,000 Americans. By 1975, the rate was 5,282 per 100,000 people.

Today the Baby Boomers are increasingly in charge of America – and a lot of people are scared.

Why?

Baby Boomers seldom understand the concept of absolute truth. We were raised being told that everything is gray – no absolute white or absolute black. Nothing is completely right or wrong. Textbooks were praised if they were "values free" – taking no position on good or evil.

As a result, I believe we are America's first completely confused and drifting generation.

Why?

Could it be that for the first time in American history, prayer was kicked out of their schools? Also, those schools after World War II finally gradually became government agencies instead of local schoolhouses run by communities.

Ours was the first generation where mandatory attendance was effectively enforced. My father did not finish school, primarily because nobody did anything about his dropping out of grade school so he could work to support his family in the mid-Depression.

But now in the 1950s and 1960s, our parents were free to drop us off at school and pursue their own interests. Then they blamed the teachers when we didn't turn out right.

Meanwhile, the teachers' hands were being tied by all the social reformers and experimenters.

As a kid, I didn't watch the news. I had no idea that it was suddenly illegal to pray at school. I wouldn't have prayed anyway. Well, I take that back – Aunt Barbara at the boys' home made me learn the Lord's Prayer and repeat it every night before I went to bed.

I am convinced now that it made a difference. In later years when I was in desperate trouble, I turned to that prayer.

But as a kid, I had no idea what was going on. I was just

having a good time – and was miserable at the same time – in a society that had decreasing limits and very little ability to cope with my rebellion.

Like I said, I didn't watch the news. I didn't read social commentary. Today, I find myself doing both and wondering how I was unfortunate enough to grow up in the first period of American history where kids were encouraged to get away with this kind of rebellion.

Vast forces were at play in America.

At the same time that prayer and Bible reading were banned from the public schools, an assault began from the other side.

Ours was the first generation targeted by a music industry unconcerned about our welfare – but instead focused on the millions of dollars that could be made selling records to us. An important key to instant riches, according to superstar Little Richard, was "Shock the parents and delight the kids."

For the first time, adolescent rebellion was profitable. There were other forces at work.

"I hate to say it, but I feel the need to acknowledge the quiet triumph of secularism in the past thirty years," commentator William F. Buckley, Jr., told *Forbes* magazine when an interviewer asked, "How has America changed between 1955 and 1995?"

By secular, Buckley meant the removal of religion from American life. "It was unreasonable to expect that there wouldn't be consequences from the assault. In my day lusty agnostics would on the least invitation happily engage in trench warfare against Christianity. But it is worse now, or such is my reading.

"The evangelists of agnosticism no longer feel the need to move their armies against what, in their judgment, is nowadays only a derelict defense force. It isn't that, of course, but the indifference to religion, reflected in the life of the university, is a development of great social consequence."

Buckley told of recently listening to the message by President

Franklin Roosevelt when he communicated to the American people that the D–Day landings in Normandy had occurred and that the reconquest of Europe was in sight.

Listen to what President Roosevelt said as America listened over the 1945 radio airwaves.

"Almighty God: Our sons, pride of our nation, this day have set upon a mighty endeavour ... They will need Thy blessings ... we know that by Thy grace, and by the righteousness of our cause, our sons will triumph ... Thy will be done, Almighty God."

Roosevelt spoke language that suggested the ultimate dimension of the human experience, and "this was the foundation of American idealism, liberty under God. Fear of God made the difference in American society," says Buckley.

Beginning with my wild generation, nobody was told to fear the Almighty.

As a result today, what Buckley calls "the great regulator of days gone by" is no longer vibrant.

And, continues the columnist, "the consequences hardly need to be enumerated. In other ages it was all there: crime, libertinism, self-centerdness, infidelity. But, it was viewed as departure from the correct standards. Now we get people such as the Surgeon General, whose answer to the question 'Is it wrong to conceive out of wedlock?' was: 'No. Everyone has different moral standards.'"

But there were so many other forces battering civilization.

"In the last fifty years 'Moral relativity' has impeded the teaching of values and ethics to our children," says Ann Landers, the popular newspaper advice columnist. "Society expects the schools to handle the upbringing of our children. Schools emphasize 'self-esteem' at the expense of personal responsibility and community obligation."

I grew up in the middle of this transition from a godly nation to where we are today – under assault by our own rebelliousness. Things are far, far worse today than when I was a kid. What we did was shocking. Our neighborhood gangs robbed and stole and raped and got high.

But when we ambushed rival street gangs, we fought with fists, chains, baseball bats, knives and occasional guns. Now, it's automatic weapons. And the violence continues to escalate.

"Youngsters used to shoot each other in the body. Then in the head," says Judge Susan R. Winfield, who presides over the Family Division of the Washington, D.C., Superior Court. "Now they shoot each other in the face. There is far more gratuitous violence and far more anger, more shooting."

Gunfire has become sufficiently common in and around classrooms, mostly in the inner city, that an astonishing number of schools are tearing out lockers to deny hiding places for handguns, according to Richard Lacayo, writing in *Time* magazine. He notes that the American juvenile-justice system was designed 100 years ago to reform kids found guilty of minor crimes.

Today that system is overwhelmed by kids, who openly defy the system to affect them. As I did.

"We need to throw out our entire juvenile-justice system," says Gil Garcetti, the District Attorney here in Los Angeles. He says his biggest headache is our city's youth gangs.

He has proposed that Los Angeles replace the juvenile system with one that both protects society from violent juvenile criminals and efficiently rehabilitates youths who can be saved — and can differentiate between the two.

How he is going to do that remains to be seen, but he tells a story that illustrates how serious the problem has become:

Speaking at a juvenile detention center, he was confronted during a question-and-answer session by a teen who asked: "If I kill someone, can I be executed?"

"Not at your age, no," said Garcetti, uneasily.

"What if I kill more than one person?"

"Under current California law, you cannot be executed."

"Right now, I'm under sixteen. If I kill someone, I get out of prison when I'm twenty-five, right – no matter what?"

"Right," said Garcetti, who cut off the kid's questions by predicting, "But people are so tired, so fearful and so disgusted that I think you're going to see some real changes in juvenile laws."

American children today – especially the teenagers among them – spend relatively tiny amounts of time with their parents – or their homework. They spend vastly greater amounts of time on other things, from crime to television, notes Bennett.

A few years ago a special commission of political, medical, educational, and business leaders issued a report on the health of America's teenagers titled *Code Blue*. In the words of this report, "Never before has one generation of American teenagers been less healthy, less cared for, or less prepared for life than their parents were at the same age."

According to the sociologist David Popenoe, today's generation of children is the first in our nation's history to be less well-off psychologically and socially than its parents.

In a free society, families, schools, and churches have a vital responsibility for shaping the character of the young. When they no longer provide moral instruction or lose their moral authority, there is very little that the federal government can do, says Bennett.

Of school, church and family, the family is the most important. Christian economist Michael Novak of the American Enterprise Institute has said that the original and best Department of Health, Education, and Welfare is the family. But the family today is an agency in disrepair.

Popenoe agrees, noting that the 1960s through to the 1990s "witnessed an unprecedented decline of the family as a social institution. Families have lost functions, social power, and authority over their members."

In only thirty years, TV shows have gone from celebrating the family through *Father Knows Best, Bonanza, The Big Valley, Leave It to Beaver, Lassie* and *The Real McCoys* to making "a virtue of promiscuity, adultery, homosexuality, and gratuitous acts of violence," according to former Secretary of Education William Bennett. "Rap music celebrates the abuse and torture of women. Advertisements are increasingly erotic, even perverse. And many of our most successful and critically-acclaimed movies celebrate brutality, casual cruelty, and twisted sex."

None of this has taken place in a moral or cultural vacuum, Bennett notes. During the last thirty years we have witnessed a profound shift in public attitudes.

We should not flinch from admitting this unsettling truth, says Bennett: "We live in a culture which seems dedicated to the corruption of the young, to assuring the loss of their innocence before their time."

"It dawned on me recently," the anthropologist David Murray writes, "that we have now become the kind of society that in the 19th century almost every Christian denomination felt compelled to missionize."

Will the federal government save society?

Between 1962 and 1992, welfare spending in the United States increased by over 900 percent in 1992 dollars. At the same time, the poverty rate dropped by less than five percent – and illegitimacy rates increased over 400 percent.

John J. Dilulio, Jr. of Princeton University, has observed: "The problem is that inner-city children are trapped in criminogenic homes, schools, and neighborhoods where high numbers of teenagers and adults are no more likely to nurture, teach, and care for children than they are to expose them to neglect, abuse, and violence ... Children cannot be socialized by adults who are themselves unsocialized (or worse), families that exist in name only, schools that do not educate, and neighborhoods in which violent and repeat criminals circulate in and out of jail..."

Do not misunderstand me. Just because American society was disintegrating around me as I entered childhood and became a teen is no excuse for my behavior.

I still had the ability to say no.

But I did not.

I was delighting in my defiance.

By the age of fifteen, I was well on my way to becoming institutionalized. By that, I mean that I was increasingly unable to function in the outside world. I did better behind bars — thriving in the social subculture there.

Ideally, a gang member of my age would have spent as long as he could out on the streets, partying with the neighborhood. Then he would get busted and would be OK about it, because he had had a lot of fun. He would have plenty of stories to tell in jail about the fights he had been in and his sexual triumphs.

But I was spending more time in jail than outside. And I didn't mind. I was never out for long enough to know what I was missing. Besides, I was young and full of energy, and time was insignificant to me.

I thought I was going to live forever.

Juvenile Hall and Youth Authority were a microcosm of what and who we would become in prison in later life. It was an extremely self-conscious time. It was also a time when some make the decision in their hearts that living behind bars was not the life for them. They were the smart ones.

It was also a time of breeding racial hatreds. Before *juvie*, I didn't hate any Blacks. There was a difference between them and me, but no hate. But locked up, we all became racists, unable to tolerate the cultural differences. We accused the Whites and Blacks of rudeness, loudness and outright disrespect. They had their own lists of accusations against us. But we were all learning to be racists.

After Paso Robles I was sent on to the Preston School of Industry. Known as "The Castle," this was a youth jail inside an old Spanish-built fort dating back to the 1790s. It looked like something out of a Dracula movie.

There, I made lots of friends. Shorty and Wino were in for

stabbing a 59-year-old man for the $40 in his wallet. On the witness stand, the man testified that Shorty had told him, "Come on, man, this is a robbery – don't make it a murder. Just give us your money." He didn't, so they stabbed him, then took his money.

Penguin, who I had known at the boys' home, was fifteen. He had robbed a 47-year-old Pomona man, beating him with a baseball bat, then taking a joy ride in his pickup.

Nico was a fifteen-year-old from San Fernando suspected of murdering the sixteen-year-old son of a Los Angeles police detective in a suburban back-yard after the cop's kid tried to reclaim the $2,500 stereo system his father had given him. Nico supposedly made a noose from guitar string and put it around the kid's neck and started pulling. The boy struggled with the noose for quite a while. Then he lay still.

Nico told me he didn't do it – that the kid had crossed a street gang, threatening to rat on them for drug sales.

After Preston I was sent on to a Youth Training School. There, I had lots of friends from the street and from the camp and Paso Robles and Preston. One was a slightly crazy guy from Santa Barbara we can call Listo – who I made friends with back at the Youth Authority camp.

Listo's mother had been an addict, his father a drug dealer. After being taken from them at age ten by social workers, Listo went to live with an aunt in East Los Angeles. His uncle, a security guard, let him shoot a .22-caliber revolver at age eleven, and Listo never forgot the feeling of power. He craved it – holding such explosive death and mayhem in his hands.

He loved guns.

By the time he was fourteen, he had a collection of guns and had discovered that a ready supply of firearms could always be found in rich people's houses. They always had a lot of ammunition, too – something difficult for a junior high schooler to buy.

Not being able to wrap his hands around a gun, I believe, was one of the things that Listo hated most about jail. He could not feel the incredible release that comes with pulling the trigger. He was a deadly shot. He could hit moving targets a football field away.

He could break down a weapon, clean it, and put it back together like a master. In jail, he would draw pictures of guns. Between stints in jail, he also began working for the Brotherhood. At first, he just sold guns to members – weapons that he heisted in burglaries. Sometimes he took orders, looking for a specific model requested.

Then, he graduated to loan-shark enforcer and did his work by shooting people in the leg – just enough to hurt them, scaring them into raising the money they owed.

One day, $2,000 he had collected was dropped or stolen in a street scuffle. Listo was furious. He had been set up – goaded into the struggle by a girl. He had been set up, he felt sure. And now he was in trouble.

Panicking, he confronted an ex-convict he suspected of having talked the girl into the scam.

"Hey, I figured if I shot him, the Brotherhood wouldn't think I'd taken the money," Listo told me. "I had to do something. *Ese*, that dude actually got on his knees and begged for his life. I shot him in the face at point-blank range and he died instantly. Blood was everywhere. Parts of his head were laying in the doorway. What is really stupid is that I didn't have to kill him. If I'd just shot him in the leg, he would have found me some money. But I was so crazy that day, I just thought, 'Ah, what the hell,' and shot him."

Listo puffed on a cigarette. His voice was a monotone. "I didn't get my money." He exhaled a cloud of smoke and stared into the darkness of the yard. "I had to rob some woman making a night deposit."

He shrugged.

Right after my eighteenth birthday, I was freed – back on the street. Had Youth Authority detention rehabilitated me? Are you kidding?

I was a hardened criminal.

I felt like I was just getting started.

At the same time, I had a lot of compassion for the underdog. I was always taking up for little guys who were being bullied.

So why did I keep getting in trouble?

With me, guys in prison were to be admired. Crime was the key to riches, fame and power.

Going to jail was just a part of my chosen profession – in which I intended to become a top gun.

CHAPTER NINE

UP FROM THE MINOR LEAGUES

To celebrate my release from the Youth Authority, I got high on barbiturates and decided that I needed to make some quick money to buy more drugs.

Getting money was easy – all I had to do was to go into a store and take it. So I did.

Unfortunately, there was a cop nearby.

Within thirty-four hours of being released I was charged with armed robbery and with being under the influence of drugs. I found myself in front of a judge who told me I was dangerous and a threat to society. None of the youth custodial institutions could contain me, he said. Because of my age and the violent nature of my crimes, the only course left open to him was to sentence me to the state penitentiary.

When I heard that I was not crushed – as you might think. I did not mourn my freedom. I was not upset. Not at all. By going to the adult prison, I was finally on my way up.

How do I explain that this is no idle brag? How can I show you? I am not sure that somebody from outside the craziness of inner-city gang life can grasp what I felt.

So they wanted to put me in prison – well, there I would finally become a major player, not just some kid on the edges. In my mind, I was moving up the major leagues. No longer was I hoping to be noticed in some farm club in the minor leagues. No longer did I hope a scout was watching.

Now I was for real.

I would be truly respected and feared now. Plus, the

California corrections system was not exactly something I held in terror. If I was being sent off to some penitentiary in the Deep South, I might have been concerned. If I had been caught and convicted in Mexico or Panama, I would be hesitant. There your relatives have to bribe their way inside just to make sure you get fed.

But I was entering America's most populous prison system with 115,000 inmates, 84,000 parolees and 315,000 employees. There are more people in the California prison system than in the entire state of Vermont.

I was at Tracy for three years, and those years were nothing more than a training course for a career as a gangster. It was a very different environment to the Youth Authority institutions. Instead of counselors, there were now prison guards, tough men you couldn't communicate with. This created a "them" and "us" mentality – especially since the guards carried guns.

The average age of inmates at Tracy was eighteen. We were all out to prove ourselves. Peer pressure was strong, and I was determined to make a good impression. I was still in the gang that the Sinners had evolved into – the notorious First Flats street gang. In Tracy, there were quite a few members there. Tracy contained members of all kinds of gangs from all over California. It wasn't unusual to find forty members of the same gang inside.

Again, street rivalries were downplayed in favor of racial differences. Each group had its own dress code. The Hispanic gang members were always dressed smartly, with creased pants and shirts buttoned only at the top. Just like the tattoos, our clothes were a statement of who and what we were. The White gangs were always in a minority – and made a big show of being badder than anybody.

They claimed to be Nazis and Ku Klux Klan members. They made a determined effort to prove it, too. They were dramatically outnumbered by the Hispanics and Blacks.

On weekends, hundreds of inmates would spill out onto the

prison yard, each race doing its own thing. In one corner, the Blacks would be listening to soul music like Marvin Gaye and James Brown.

Johnny Cash and Hank Williams would blare from the White corner. We Hispanics, you might be surprised to hear, did not play marimba music or samba or salsa. No mariachis and sombreros for us – that's for the benefit of camera-toting tourists. We would play what we called "oldies but goodies" music – smooth hits from the 1950s and 1960s.

There was a strong feeling of comradeship among each group and a war mentality toward the others. The gangs like the White Supremacists would study Hitler and the Ku Klux Klan and sport swastika tattoos.

The Blacks were into Malcolm X and Black Islam, and the Zulu warriors of South Africa. The Hispanics idolized revolutionaries like Pancho Villa and Emilo Zapata and the Aztec leader Cuatemoc, and we used to talk about "taking the land back" – reconquering California and the other parts of the United States which had once belonged to Mexico.

The presence of so many rival gangs in such a confined space produced an atmosphere of intense hatred and violence. Riots and race fights broke out all the time, and people weren't fighting each other with fists any more.

They were getting stabbed with knives or hit over the head with pipes. I had come into Tracy thinking I was a super-bad dude who could take on anybody, but when I saw how quickly and easily someone could get killed or badly injured there, I realized just how vulnerable I was – like everyone else. Fist-fighting and kick-fighting on the streets had been exciting, but I was taken aback to see death and maiming at such close range. Some of the deaths were silent and swift.

Others were loud and bloody.

I found myself in with guys who bragged about killing – and told what had gone wrong with hits that they messed up. It was like attending a 24-hour-a-day crime academy.

For example, a skinny, very talkative guy named Paco bragged to me that when he was twelve, he slammed his first heroin, and soon was committing burglaries and stealing cars. He claimed that he killed for the first time at age thirteen, when he stabbed a rival in the neck.

"*Orale, ese,* I done capped many drug dealers, thugs and garbage," he told me. "Ain't no thing. You are ridding the world of another piece of trash." As I looked around me, it made sense.

Paco told me how he would wear gloves that concealed a 9-mm. pistol at the ready in his right hand, and a knife in the left.

Gang-fashion, the gloves had had their fingers snipped off. That way the knife or gun could be pushed forward, ready to use, in an instant.

It was important, he said, to put targets at ease and then strike when they were convinced you were their friend. He told me about stalking a major player in the drug trade around Van Nuys Boulevard.

Paco watched as the dealer went into a warehouse. His name was on the *lista* – meaning he had been condemned to death – for killing a drug courier rather than paying him.

Before following him inside, Paco bought a bottle of Jack Daniels. Inside, he found the dealer just relaxing against a wall, smoking a cigarette. Paco bummed a smoke off of him and offered him a sip of whiskey.

Then, he sat down and after the two had traded sips for a while, the man relaxed and began talking about his teenage sons. With the dealer's defenses down, Paco stuck his knife first into the man's heart, then his throat.

Then Paco walked away from the corpse, being careful to take the fingerprint-laden wine bottle with him.

The story surprised me.

But I was careful not to let anyone see that I was stunned by the culture of hard-core violence that surrounded me. I knew I couldn't show any sign of weakness. Here, the weak were spat upon, humiliated and made into miserable slaves. Their money and their manhood would be stripped from them and they would be used in terrible ways.

Sex was a tool for some of these guys. The worst predators were not romantic or even really homosexual. Instead, sex was a way to humiliate, dominate, control and terrify.

Young, experienced *vatos locos* like myself fought by being above that kind of thing. I fought back by being intensely loyal and completely straightforward with my friends. In return, they were totally loyal to me.

We fought common enemies. We did unto others before they did unto us. I thought I could win every contest by simply never giving anyone else a chance.

I studied body language, always ready to defend myself by attacking a split second before the other guy made his move.

I watched the older guys and followed their example. I observed a samurai-like code of honor: never show fear; never back down from a fight; never let your manhood be taken by a sexual predator; always stick with your gang and your race – and never inform, never.

If you "ratted" you would end up either dead or living a miserable life in fear.

By obeying this code you would win respect from your fellow gang members. And then you might live.

There were unwritten laws of prison survival, and the most important law was to be armed at all times.

Fights could flare up at any moment, and we had to be ready. That meant depending on your friends, but never being solely dependent on them. You could only depend on yourself.

But it was important to have a weapon with which to defend yourself.

Since the guards often conducted cell shake-downs and strip searches, staying armed meant stashing as many weapons as you could in different places around the prison.

And you spent a lot of time making weapons.

CHAPTER TEN

FROM SOLEDAD TO SAN QUENTIN

Weapons can be made out of anything in prison. Sharpened spoons are deadly.

Some guys take a piece of steel, say from a bedframe and draw the shape of a knife onto it with a paper clip.

Then they patiently, carefully trace over and over and over the outline, scratching out just a little more metal each time until a knife shape is cut out. It then is sharpened carefully on the rough concrete floor, honed until razor sharp.

In Tracy prison, I began to hear murmurs about the Brotherhood. Nobody talked openly about it but you knew that it was there and that it wielded a lot of power.

Being a member of the Mafia was the ultimate for a kid like me. Out on the streets I had suffered the sting of racism. Limitations had been imposed on me because I was Hispanic and born poor.

But inside Tracy prison there were guys from the same sort of background as mine who had broken through those barriers and had become somebody important. Only the baddest of the bad from every neighborhood were allowed into the Brotherhood.

It was a special breed, an elite organization, feared and respected by everyone. To be a member was my dream.

I started getting into fights to build up my reputation. I deliberately looked for action, trying to make a point. I became known for being wherever there was trouble.

I spent a lot of time in segregation – "the hole," where you were sent for punishment. It was a noisy place, 24 hours a day, full of young guys like me.

We were scarcely men yet, but we were so aggressively violent that the system had to create special ways to keep us in line.

I would be locked up in the hole for twenty-nine days, and then California law stipulated that after this a psychiatrist had to talk to me. The psychological assessments were always the same.

Even at the age of fourteen I had been described as "abnormal," "sociopathic," "anti-social," "psychopathic" and "suffering from delusions of grandeur."

I would boast to the psychologist that my gang was the toughest in the world, that I was the meanest dude in the world and that no one could beat me in a fight. The psychiatrists would observe me bragging or fighting and would conclude that it was because I was emotionally disturbed, but in fact I was just proving myself and establishing myself. What they labeled as anti-social behavior was just survival in my eyes.

I felt there was no point in talking to psychiatrists, so I used to play with them. They would ask me all sorts of searching questions, and I would give them the answers they were expecting.

"What would you do if you got home and discovered that someone had raped your sister?" they would ask.

"I'd kill him," I would reply.

"What would you do if you got home and discovered that someone had –"

"Don't even think about talking about my Mama," I would shout. "I'll kill you!"

They would scribble it all down on their reports. Then they would show me different images and would ask me what I saw in them. To tease them, my answers were always violent. "That looks like somebody being stabbed," I would say. "This one is somebody's head coming off. That one looks like somebody's guts spilling out."

I would only talk to them if they gave me a cigarette. When I had finished smoking I would stop talking. They had to give me another if we were to continue.

As I got older they began to describe me as cold and ruthless, a danger to society. One psychiatrist said I would never be able to maintain human relationships.

Talking to them was so dull that I found myself playing games with them. Well, you can imagine the conclusions they drew. I was declared dangerous and volatile.

I was still only eighteen when I was told that I was going to receive electric shock treatment. This process kills the front part of the brain and supposedly made you less violent.

They have since discovered the treatment didn't actually work. The same was true of lobotomy, where the front part of the brain was removed by surgery.

But thousands of men were turned into walking vegetables by these treatments before they were stopped. I thank God that I was under twenty-one years of age and the authorities needed the permission of my relatives to carry out the electrotherapy.

My Aunt Margaret refused to sign the paper.

At Tracy I met guys who had been there for five or seven years. This was sobering. I wondered if I would be in for as long as that.

Often inmates at Tracy would be back in jail again mere months or even weeks after being released. But the really smart guys were the ones who didn't come back. They had thought about the prospect of a lifetime in and out of jail, and had decided it wasn't for them. So they found steady jobs, got married and raised families.

I would hear about guys like that and I would envy them, knowing that they had done the right thing, wishing deep down that I had done the same thing myself.

Many of the men at Tracy had regular visits from girlfriends or wives and children. My family never came to see me. I wrote to a few of the girls I had liked, but I was already preparing myself to do without them, knowing that I would probably be inside for years.

As the late 1960s and early 1970s were a time of radical social change in the United States – with a revolutionary attitude among the young people throughout the whole country – this rebellion found its way into the prisons.

Some inmates took up causes – such as *La Revolución,* the idea that the U.S. government might be overthrown and a Hispanic regime put in its place, at least in California.

I was never much of a revolutionary, however. Other people's beliefs sparked many prison riots, with fatalities among both the inmates and the guards.

Because I was too much of a trouble-maker at Tracy, I was transferred to Soledad State Prison in 1973, which was a bigger prison with tighter security.

I was only there for a while, but Soledad – or "Gladiator School," as it was called – served as a more advanced training ground in violence and gangland culture.

It was there that I saw first-hand how rival gangs sometimes worked together. For example, there was the slaying of a convicted Nevada mob hit man which everybody said was a contract hit ordered by Italian mobsters.

But it was executed by members of a rival gang. Out in the exercise yard, the Italian guy was struck in the back of the head with a pipe and stabbed seventeen times. One guy walked behind him, swinging that pipe and two other brothers walked up in front and on both sides, stabbing like crazy, in and out, in and out, in and out. He was dead before he hit the ground.

Why was he hit?

Some said it was out of revenge. There was another rumor that he had become a federal informant, but that wasn't it. He was a hit man, and had killed as many as thirty people, supposedly burying most of them in a bird sanctuary.

But the real reason he died in our exercise yard was that he had gotten "reckless and sloppy," and people close to him were afraid of what he might do next.

He was at Soledad on a parole violation, but actually had been picked up on suspicion of attacking a crime figure in Hollywood with a shotgun as the target sat in a restaurant after celebrating the fourth birthday of a friend's granddaughter.

The target was blasted "multiple times" in the head, neck and chest by blasts from outside a glassed-in atrium.

However, the target lived.

The four-year-old and other members of the party had just left the restaurant, and the girl's elderly grandmother had moved to another table with friends. So, for mere seconds, the target had been sitting alone, reading the *Wall Street Journal*. About ten shotgun blasts were fired through the plate glass. Complete pandemonium erupted in the restaurant as customers were hit by flying glass and buckshot.

Here is what caught my attention. Buckshot disperses when it goes through glass. By firing through a window, the shooter would certainly hit the target, but not necessarily kill him. So this guy had gotten sloppy.

He was a former boxer, so maybe he was losing his grip. I believe his mob cohorts were not sure what he would mess up next.

So they gave him early retirement.

They had contacts inside Soledad who put in a request. Gang members were asked to return a favor.

Out of professional courtesy, they complied.

After Soledad, I was moved to Vacaville State Prison for the Criminally Insane.

What an insult! I guess I had played too many mind games with the prison psychologists.

Vacaville was a wild place. At one point they experimented with a medical program to curb violence, using drugs like Quaaludes, Valium and Thorazine. The drugs were greatly enjoyed by the inmates, but the program failed after a death and multiple stabbings were discovered to have centered around trafficking in those temporarily "legal" substances.

Then, I was moved to San Quentin State Prison, a very large

maximum security prison with 5,000 inmates. The men there were doing long time, from five years to life. Deep within the prison was Death Row and the gas chamber.

San Quentin was the home of the famous cult murderer Charles Manson and of Sirhan Bishara Sirhan, the assassin of Senator Robert F. Kennedy.

And now me.

I was twenty-three years old.

CHAPTER ELEVEN
FOREVER DAMNED

I remember the journey from Soledad, to San Quentin over the San Raphael Bridge. Inside the prison bus, men were shackled together by their wrists and ankles. Through the barred windows I looked out and felt a deep longing for the outside world – from which I would soon be cut off for a very long time. Many of the men in that bus never left San Quentin, except in a pine box.

When we arrived at the prison, the first thing I noticed was the gun tower. It was 100 feet high and equipped with a .50-caliber machine gun. We checked in at Receiving and Release and were given our prison issue clothing – white uniforms with "S.Q." on the back. We were then led into the yard, an enclosure of about three acres. As we entered, I became aware of a deep humming sound, which at first I couldn't identify. Then I recognized it as the drone of thousands of male voices echoing off the huge cell blocks.

We, the newcomers, walked through the yard in single file. All eyes were on us. I did my best to present an air of defiance, but inside I felt apprehensive, wondering what was in store for me and hoping I could rise to the challenge.

The Brotherhood knew in advance that I was coming. They ran most of the drug trafficking inside, and with some of their profits they paid for such things as checking the records of incoming prisoners, so they knew who to expect.

When I arrived my reputation as a gangster had preceded me. The Brotherhood saw me as a bad dude with immense potential. So I found myself befriended by a mixture of new and old friends.

Mafia members were well-dressed men with tattoos and mustaches. They carried themselves with dignity and they were feared and respected by everyone in the prison. They lived by a simple but deadly code: "Blood in, blood out." You had to kill to get in, and you only got out when you died.

The black hand of death was their symbol.

To qualify for membership, you had to undergo a screening process. First of all they would check your record and make sure you had never raped a woman, molested a child or betrayed your gang. Also, no homosexuals were accepted.

Next, you had to prove your courage, and above all your loyalty to the organization. Allegiance to the Brotherhood had to come before loyalty to your family. You had to be prepared to kill for it.

I was asked to carry out a "move" on an enemy of the brotherhood. This was the final part of my initiation.

A murder.

I tried to react casually when I was told, as if "booking" someone was the most natural thing in the world. "Sure, no problem," I said as they pointed out the victim.

But that night, when I was alone in my cell, my mind was in a whirl. I had been asked to kill a human being in cold blood, eyeball to eyeball, and I didn't want to do it. I didn't even know the guy.

Even at that stage in my life, after all the violence I had been involved in, I was aware of how inhuman this act would be. It was a very different thing from shooting someone in the frenzy of a gang fight or while under the influence of drugs.

I paced back and forth, weighing up my options. I could go back and admit that I had changed my mind, that I couldn't go through with it.

But then I would lose all credibility and respect, which would set me on a downward spiral. There was no telling what might happen to me after that. On the other hand, what if I went through with it and made a mistake? What if the hit was armed? What if I was shot by one of the guards?

I spent all night thinking about it, wrestling with myself. I had to make a decision.

Lots of murders happen in American prisons.

The victim is minding his own business in his cell. Somebody walks past. The victim looks up and is suddenly doused with a flammable liquid. Before he has a chance to cry out, somebody else walks past the cell and holds a lit match in front of an aerosol can – creating a flame thrower, igniting the thrown liquid. The victim is turned into a screaming human torch. Often the victim survives – although horribly and permanently scarred, possibly blinded. In terrible pain and in the safety of a hospital, he may well decide to identify his attackers.

Often times, a victim steps out of his cell. Suddenly, from behind a cord tightens around his throat, strangling him as it cuts off his air and the blood to his brain. The victim dies quickly, but usually puts up a heroic struggle.

Death may take a couple of minutes, during which the victim may thrash about loudly and even manage to yell for help. In his final second, he will struggle to make eye contact with you, pleading with you to have mercy. You cannot. His first act would be to kill you.

There are dozens of other ways.

A lot of suicide hangings are actually executions. One of the most common ways to go is when a victim feels the vicious thrust of a homemade stiletto knife plunged into his chest to the hilt, penetrating his heart. The blade is plunged in rapidly, again and again. The victim usually dies. Even if found and treated quickly, the internal trauma is usually so massive that the bleeding cannot be stopped.

How many inmates die each year in U.S. prisons? Nobody seems to agree.

No one takes into account mystery deaths that occur each

year. Their causes are officially classified as "unknown." These often include unsolved or unreported murders. In prison it is rarely possible to determine who has committed suicide as opposed to who has been murdered.

Another unknown is the number of convictions for inmate murders. "State records are nonexistent or buried beneath layers of bureaucracy," reported journalist Amy Lamey in an article in *The New Republic* magazine. "When I asked for California's conviction total, a spokesman for the state's correction system told me, 'I don't know how I would get that. I'd have to find out what prisons they [the homicides] were in.'"

When she asked about getting Florida figures, a prison official there told her, "It would take some doing. You'd have to call health services."

No one tracks conviction rates for prison murders at the national level. Why are there no accurate figures on inmate murders?

"No one cares," says Virginia Prisons Administrator, Joanne Terlep.

And so it was with very little risk of being caught that I went through with my assignment – and found myself accepted by a brotherhood of murderers that accepted only murderers. A club of the eternally damned.

I looked at myself in the mirror.

I still looked the same, but I felt different.

I do not like thinking about it. I was forever damned. And I knew it. It changed me. But the guys in the Brotherhood knew that it would.

That is why they required blood to flow.

I had to buy my life in the Brotherhood with that of another. I have no idea what he did to be chosen for death. I had no grudge against him.

I was not charged with his death.

There was no evidence against me.

My victim became one more faceless statistic. Another dead

convict.

One less mouth to feed at the state's expense.

One less body to house in a cell.

CHAPTER TWELVE

BLOOD IN, BLOOD OUT

From that time on I was known as a person to be feared and respected. I was praised by my peers for what I had done, and with their praise came the conviction that I had been justified in what I had done. He had been an enemy of the Brotherhood, so of course I had done the right thing in killing him.

But something began to die within me: I learned how to flick a switch and shut off all feeling.

As the years went by in San Quentin I lost all capacity to cry or feel compassion. I gradually became inhuman, a brutal animal.

After "taking care of business," I used to feel good about a job well done.

I would sleep like a baby.

I was proud of my competence and efficiency.

That pride was constantly reinforced by the men around me. I had become a cold-blooded assassin, and I was happy with the path I had chosen.

I made a lot of enemies in San Quentin, so I had to watch my back constantly. I slept very lightly, knowing that an attack could come through the bars of my cell at any time, day or night. Sometimes the prison guards would set me up by putting me in a section with a rival gang. They would turn a blind eye to the brutality that would follow.

My strategy of defending myself by reacting first saved me from countless injuries and potentially lethal attacks, but there were a number of close calls.

On one occasion I was even stabbed in the heart, although the knife penetrated no further than the heart muscle. Luckily the knife was tubular and I saw the attack coming, so I was able to stop the knife with one hand and hit out at the attacker with my other hand.

The element of surprise was crucial. In such close quarters everybody was studying each other's body language and trying to get the edge. Some guys would talk and smile a lot before making a hit. The target would become relaxed, and then the killer would suddenly strike. I learned how to be poker-faced, always watching and aware of every movement, because a split second's lapse could be a dead give-away, turning an easy hit into a fight for my life.

Prison is a bad place.

I became a hard man.

I was known as a man of few words. Some things are better left alone. I can only share about my own personal experiences while in no way jeopardizing anyone else. As I tell you this, the story of my life, there are periods of time that we will just leave blank. We must leave some of this slate unwritten upon. I will not talk of many things.

Ugly things.

Hard things.

Evil things of which I am not proud.

I was not a happy man. I would unnerve people with my silence. But silence can be a powerful thing. If I wanted to get information out of someone I would just look at them and say nothing. They would quickly become nervous and usually would start rattling on and on, trying to break the ice. Very quickly, they would tell me what I wanted to know.

I was in prison for many years, and because I couldn't change the system or fight it, I tried to keep in good physical and mental shape to live with it. I used to see men lose their minds trying to look for a way out of prison.

I played chess and exercised my body.

This was the zenith of my faith in the Mafia. The Marine Corps has their code *Semper Fidelis* — "always faithful" to Corps, Unit, God, and Country. Mine was The Brotherhood *primero y ultimo hasta la tumba!* — which translates as "The Brotherhood first and last until the grave!"

The Marines feel that the worst thing in the world is to break rank or rat on your brother. It was the same with the Mafia. However, we took it several steps further. It turned into almost a religion requiring celibacy and suicidal sacrifice, kind of like a Catholic monk and a Kamikaze blended into one, bringing forth a devoted, focused killer who believed he was morally right!

I read a lot of books, particularly about anatomy. I would draw a life-sized diagram of the human body on the wall, and I would sketch in the organs in their proper places. That was my entertainment! It also helped me in my "work," since it taught me exactly where to strike so as to be most effective.

For escapism I would read books about foreign countries and travel around the world in my imagination. I also read about historical figures such as Julius Caesar, Napoleon, Mao, Hitler, Mussolini, Al Capone and Lucky Luciano. I was fascinated by violent, strong men. They became my role models.

One book I never read was the Bible. To me, biblical characters and stories were in the same category as Greek myths. I thought of belief in God as something strictly for children and old people.

Groups of Christians would visit the prison every now and then. They would come on to my tier with their guitars and sing songs at me while I was trying to sleep. They were not only irritating, but it looked bad for me to have Christians singing outside my cell. I wanted to make sure that no one thought I was encouraging them, so I used to throw hot coffee at them and swear until they would leave. I would threaten to kill them if they ever came to my tier again.

But one night, out of the blue, the Lord's Prayer suddenly

came into my mind. I was so startled that I jumped out of bed! Aunt Barbara had forced me to memorize it all those years ago, and it was still there.

Why had I recalled it so clearly after all that time? As I thought about it I felt a sense of peace come over me, and I slept soundly.

I was always involved in trouble at San Quentin. During my time there I went from the general prison population into disciplinary segregation and on to isolation – what in the movies they call solitary confinement.

There I was locked up for many months in a "strip cell." I was given only underwear, no bedding, a cement slab to sleep on and a hole in the ground for a toilet. The cell was sound-proofed with triple doors. It was dark and cold and I was trapped, with no one but myself for company. I was surrounded by steel and concrete. I had no distractions or entertainment – no radio, no TV. I was allowed one hour per day to shower and exercise, which consisted mainly of walking back and forth.

I was fed only bread and water, then one proper meal every third day – delivered through a slot in the door. We were forbidden to speak with other prisoners.

My one pleasure was looking out of my cell window at a hill in the distance. When the sunlight was on it, it looked beautiful. That hill was my daily thrill. On days when it was overcast and the hill was gloomy, my mood would be glum all day.

However, being in isolation was no guarantee of safety from attack. Enemies would avenge hits or stabbings by throwing into my cell paper sacks filled with feces and urine – which broke on impact and splattered all over me, my bed, the floor and the walls.

The guards would just watch and laugh. I would have to live with the filth and stench, seething with hate, plotting my revenge.

You think all kinds of thoughts when you're alone in the stinking dark – hungry and cold, pacing back and forth all day long.

As time went on in isolation I found myself noticing cracks and flaws in the Brotherhood I had never seen before. There was jealousy, treachery and treason. Members were fighting each other and messing around with each other's wives.

My eyes were being opened to the abyss I was living in. I began to feel trapped in San Quentin's inferno of hate and violence. But even to discuss this with anyone would be to show weakness. That was a luxury I couldn't afford, so I kept all these thoughts to myself.

I didn't get many visitors during those long, dark years in prison. Sometimes girlfriends would drop off some money and drugs. My rule was never to get involved emotionally. I saw the anguish that some of the other guys suffered at visiting time. There would be an inch-thick screen of bullet-proof glass between them and their loved ones. They would be so very close to each other but yet so far, unable to touch.

At the end of visiting time, the prisoner would have to watch his family go out into the sunshine of the outside world, while he would be handcuffed and taken back into the darkness of the prison.

I often used to think about life outside prison. I yearned to have the freedom just to go for a walk in the park and to be able to keep on walking, without anyone telling me, "Stop! That's far enough!"

I wanted to be able to do what I wanted, with the light on or off – whatever I wanted – and no one to say, "Get back in your cell. Lights out!" I longed for a life free of the slamming of steel doors, boxing me in, denying me freedom.

I wanted to have some privacy, to live in my own home. I was sick of being told when to wake up, when to shower, when to go to sleep. I longed for some real Hispanic food – not the bland prison fare I had to endure.

I wanted the freedom to get in a car and go anywhere and see anyone I pleased. I used to dream about going to an all-night restaurant to eat pancakes. I would imagine resting in the grass on a sunny day and getting up in the middle of the night to watch television and eat a snack and going down the street to buy a burger, any time I wanted to.

These were the simple pleasures and freedoms I dreamed of, and I hoped that I would be able to enjoy all of them again one day. The loss of these things is what makes a prison a prison. A person appreciates the joys of life more when they are taken away. However, it never occurred to me the loss of lives, pain and destruction that I had brought about.

After eleven years in prison, I was released from San Quentin.

This was certainly not due to good behavior on my part. A new law that was part of the Prisoner's Bill of Rights had recently been passed in the Senate in California.

Its purpose was to reduce overcrowding in prisons, and it stipulated an automatic review of all prison sentences which were indeterminate rather than fixed.

My sentence had been seven years to life, and the authorities decided that under the terms of the new law I was actually overdue for release by five years. Because of this legal loop-hole, they had no choice but to let me go – although I had picked up three more felony convictions while behind bars, and even though the prison had a long list of "silent" complaints against me for suspected crimes!

The authorities at San Quentin were furious. The lieutenant in charge of me was so angry that he made me spend the last six months before my release date in solitary confinement in the strip cells. I just laughed at him, knowing that there was no way they could keep me down now that I was so close to freedom.

"We'll keep a cell for you, Blajos!" he warned me. "You'll be back here – and real soon!"

"Don't hold your breath waiting for me!" I laughed back.

On the day of my release I was handcuffed all the way from the prison to the local airport, where a plush airliner waited to take me back to East Los Angeles and home.

What a culture shock!

Mere hours before, I had been in a strip cell in a world full of violence and hatred. Now a pretty flight attendant was smiling down at me and asking, "Would you like a drink, sir?"

I smiled with satisfaction as I sipped the first of many celebration toasts to myself. I was a free man at last!

Eleven years is a long time to spend in prison. As I returned to East L.A., I realized that a lot of things had changed.

The world had advanced more than a decade without me. I was almost thirty years old.

I was a very dangerous and capable man, and physically at the peak of my manhood. Even so, I was socially backward, with the same immature mentality I had possessed when I had first gone into Tracy prison all those years ago at age eighteen.

I had told no one I was coming home, so no one was at the airport waiting for me. I wanted it this way. Some guys had their wives and friends and family. Not me. The fewer who knew, the better. I knew the power of secrecy and independence. It was a way of life, sort of an ongoing celebration of death as we prepared to die all the time.

I went straight to the home of one of my brothers in the Mafia. I wanted him to give me the *lista* – the roster of guys denounced for death. I asked him for a gun. I was offering myself with no strings attached. My sole desire was to do my duty for the organization.

I thought of myself as a soldier.

The only thing I was interested in was eliminating my enemies, and if it meant I had to sacrifice my freedom and go straight back into prison, that was okay. But I was determined to kill two or three enemies of the Brotherhood before I went back in.

The corners of the brother's mouth began to curl up and twitch with humor as he listened to me. I stood there, deadly earnest, trying to figure out why he thought I was funny.

I had spent eleven years locked in a cell, learning how to hate and kill, and this man wasn't taking me seriously! He suggested that I should try to lighten up a little.

I took his advice, but it wasn't easy at first. Although I had reluctantly become an assassin at the beginning, by now it was something I felt I had to do whether I liked it or not.

I didn't know how to be or do anything else. Consequently I felt at a loss in normal society. I had forgotten how to have relationships. I didn't know how to relate to my friends and family.

The world outside had changed so much that I hardly recognized it. Cars were a lot smaller than I remembered. Planes were a lot bigger.

Fashions and hairstyles were different, but that didn't matter much to me, as I still dressed like a homeboy. The computer age had arrived in earnest, and the leap in technology made me feel as if I had stepped out of a time warp. Making a phone call was a frustration to me, because I had never used a push-button phone before. When I tried to buy a car, I was told they wouldn't accept cash.

I had stepped unprepared into an age of plastic money, and credit cards were a real headache to me. Of course, any that I had were from the robberies that I began pulling to support myself.

And credit cards were traceable.

They could get you into serious trouble.

But it was worth all the frustrations just to be a free man. I enjoyed being able to do all the little things I had dreamed of back in prison.

I should have realized just how precious that freedom was.

I should have cleaned up my act, gotten a real job, worked hard and raised a family. But I was still committed to the Brotherhood, and so there was always a chance that I would end up in jail again, steel doors slamming behind me and chains rattling. So I decided to make the most of the time I had.

I intended to make a lot of money.

CHAPTER THIRTEEN

A BRIEF TASTE OF FREEDOM

It was good to be back again in Boyle Heights, my old neighborhood. Everybody knew I had been in San Quentin, so the local homeboys rolled out the red carpet and treated me like a celebrity.

Those first days home, the neighborhood boys followed me around, hanging on my every word. I was a big fish in a little bowl.

"We heard about you, Conejo," they would say. "Are you really in the Brotherhood?"

So I would tell them what life was like in prison, and they would look up at me with awe, hanging on my every word, especially my stories about the fights I had been in. As I looked down at these kids, they reminded me very much of myself, fifteen years before.

They were becoming involved in the gangster culture, just as I had done. Their questions told me loud and clear that what they really wanted was to be just like me. Here was a whole new generation looking for someone or something to believe in, to follow with faith and commitment.

They had no lack of loyalty or courage. They were willing and ready to serve someone with their lives. A lot of them already had gun-shot or stab wounds. They had learned at an early age that as members of the gang culture, they should expect to spend at least five or ten years in jail.

Their manhood depended on it.

They would have done anything I had told them to do,

112

knowing that it would put them in good standing with me and so with the Brotherhood. I was struck by the realization that I had real power over these boys – a power greater than money or guns.

They were willing to give their very lives for a cause. These intense, courageous young men saw me as a role model, as the sort of man they wanted to become. And there I stood among them, having fulfilled every dream I had dreamed at their age. I was a living demonstration to them of what they could become.

I was a real live member of the Mafia. So I began to disciple the young men into its ways.

There was no shortage of pretty homegirls in the neighborhood, but I wasn't prepared to take them seriously or to confide in them.

I didn't want to get emotionally involved.

The German philosopher Friedrich Nietzsche – whom I read in prison – once wrote, "To fall in love is the weakness of a warrior," and those words became a motto for me. It was likely that I would end up in jail again – it went with the territory. To be in jail and to have to worry about a woman on the outside was doubly bad. You could sit and stew over questions with no answers: "What is she doing? Is she spending time with other men? Is she being faithful? Are my friends cutting in on my action?"

That was what we called "hard time" or "dirty time" in prison.

We used to ridicule the guys who talked a lot about their wives or girlfriends and wrote too many letters to them. I thought falling in love was bad for business: I knew it would distract me from serving the Brotherhood.

But after eleven years it was good to have women around, and not just for sex. Their voices were pleasantly different to men's. Their laughter had a delightful melody to it.

I had been surrounded by men for so long that spending time with a beautiful, funny woman was like standing in the sunshine or in a cool, refreshing breeze.

But I had one problem with women — it went against all my warrior instincts to sleep with a body next to mine. I would awake with a start and terrify the woman I was with. My girlfriends all ended up in bed alone, because I would go sleep on the couch. I was embarrassed that in my sleep I would push them off onto the floor.

One afternoon I went with Jenny, one of my girlfriends, to an amusement park. I was struck by the color and beauty of the place, and I enjoyed watching all the different people milling around. But my inbred instincts reacted to sudden movements. So all the action made me nervous. Even Frisbees caught my attention, and kids rushing past me on skateboards made me tense.

Jenny and I went to a little amphitheater where a hundred or so people were watching a bird show. There were little cages and cars, and the birds were performing on them, or flying off and landing on the trainer's arm. Everyone else was fascinated, but I thought it was the most stupid thing I had ever seen.

The trainer called out a command, and one of the birds jumped into a car. Another bird pulled the cart along, and the crowd erupted with laughter. But to me it sounded like a frightening roar. The sound of all those people laughing at once was so foreign that it really scared me.

As I looked around, all I could see were teeth and eyes crinkling with laughter. I thought, *these people are weird!* Then I looked at Jenny, who was laughing along with everyone else, and I thought, *you're just as weird as they are!*

"Let's get out of here!" I said and I stormed out of the amphitheater.

Jenny thought I was crazy. I thought it over later, and I realized that there was something seriously wrong with my inability to laugh. Those people had been almost rolling in the aisles with frivolity. They were all having a hilarious time, except me. I couldn't understand what was so funny.

I couldn't really relate to Jenny after that. This sense of disorientation made me want to make up for lost time. I felt a sense of urgency. I had to do something to catch up.

Money was my answer. It always solved all my problems. To make money I needed some money to begin with, so I had to find a fast way to get it. The easiest way to make instant money was to rip off big drug dealers. Robbing a bank was not a wise move: it was a federal crime which carried a long sentence. Robbing drug dealers was best, since they couldn't call the police. It was very dangerous work, but the rewards were high. It was exciting too, and it was a good way to prove myself and maintain my name on the street.

Taking chances and carrying out daring acts earned a man respect. One of my first and biggest scores came about when a friend, who I had known in prison, told me he needed my help.

His sister Irene had been cheated in a big way by a drug dealer and she wanted revenge.

In return for my help she was happy for me to keep whatever I could take in drugs or money. I had heard Irene's name mentioned from time to time as a good drug connection, someone who could be trusted.

So I agreed to talk to her.

We met over breakfast, and I studied her face and body language carefully as she told me her plan. She was green eyed and quite beautiful, but I was more impressed by how business-like and professional she was. She dealt in drugs, but wasn't addicted to them.

I respected that. I decided that she would be a useful contact. We met once more to discuss the plan further over dinner and a little cocaine. Working out the finer points of a sting-robbery like this excited me, especially when we were talking about ripping off kilos of coke with a value of about $80,000!

I could tell that she was attracted to me and although she was pretty aggressive about getting to know me, I didn't feel threatened. I liked her.

Assertiveness was a quality I valued in a woman — as long as she didn't get too nosy! I liked her courage, too. To get her revenge, she was willing to put herself on the line as bait in what was a very risky and dangerous scheme.

The plan was that Irene would first of all go to the drug dealer's house and set up a deal, offering to buy an ounce of cocaine for a couple of thousand dollars to show that she meant business.

We met up afterwards and she was able to tell me the layout of the place, where the alarms were, how many gunmen I would have to deal with, and so on.

Then I made a call to a brother who I knew would be right for the job. He was a good *pistolero* or gunman, and was someone on whom I knew I could rely.

The dealer's house was half-day's drive away, so the three of us had some fun on the way, eating at good restaurants, spending money, having a good time. This was important, because we knew that the good times could come to a very quick end if anything went wrong with the sting. We all could end up in jail or even dead.

We arrived on time, and my man went around the back of the house while Irene and I approached the door.

I made sure that Irene was in front of me, because I had been set up before and I didn't know her well enough to be sure that this was not a trap. If there was any shooting, I would use her as my shield.

Irene had already warned the dealer that she would have one of her own people with her, and I knew that he would have his own armed man inside to keep an eye on me. They knew I would be armed, but they didn't know about my *pistolero*, outside waiting for my signal to burst in and catch them unawares.

Irene had established a rapport with the dealer and he trusted her, so his defenses weren't up. From the information Irene had given me I knew where the money and drugs were, and so while she used her beauty and charm to put the dealer and his man at ease, I got ready to strike.

As we had planned, Irene casually asked the dealer if he and his two men were with the Brotherhood. This was my cue. I slapped her face, telling her to shut up, and she dropped to the floor, screaming. I aimed my gun at the dealer, and my *pistolero* burst in through the back door with his sawed-off shotgun cocked and aimed at the dealer's nearest gunman. I quickly disarmed the other.

We told them to lay face down on the floor, and we covered their mouths and bound their hands and feet with duct tape. My man and I grabbed all the money, drugs and jewelry we could find around the place and bolted out the door.

Irene, her face by now bloody and swollen, walked out in front of us, swearing at me for double-crossing her. We casually walked back to the car. I turned to wave up at the window, although no one was looking, I even honked the horn as I drove away!

In the car, $80,000 richer than we had been just half an hour before, we congratulated ourselves on a job well done. Irene had performed superbly. We also scored on some beautiful jewelry. I let her keep most of it. She had played her part so convincingly that she would never be suspected of being involved in the sting – let alone of having planned the whole thing.

The sweetness of revenge and her share of the take made the pain of her swollen face worth it. Mentioning the Mafia was all part of the plan, too. The dealer would get the idea that Irene had been double-crossed by the Brotherhood, which would enhance its reputation as an organization to be feared.

It had been a good day's work!

CHAPTER FOURTEEN

A MASTERFUL FRAME-UP

In the back of my mind, I was thinking that if I ever ended up in jail again, this sting would make a good "trip" or story to tell my brothers. Soon after this, I established myself with some big drug connections and was making a good profit as a dealer.

Also, I sent some of my money back to the prisons to take care of my brothers there. My loyalty was still strong, and taking care of the men on the inside was an important part of the code of ethics.

I was not taking any drugs myself. I didn't need to – my biggest fix was the danger and excitement of the underworld lifestyle. I had never used hard drugs in prison either, just a little marijuana now and then. It was vital to me to be disciplined so that I could serve the Brotherhood. I didn't want my perception of reality distorted.

I hated that feeling of diminished capacity, of not being in complete control of my faculties.

So, four months after my release from San Quentin, life felt good.

I had plenty of money, a growing drug business, a new car and beautiful girls. Just the mention of the Brotherhood or my name would open doors for me.

One phone call would secure me finances, or the death of an enemy, if I so wished. I felt very comfortable in my old neighborhood, treated with fear and respect. I had lost eleven years in prison, but since my release I had gained so much power and admiration that the loss seemed worth it.

Yes, I felt that crime definitely paid.

One evening, two brothers and I were at a house, waiting for the guy who lived there to come home and complete a drug deal with us.

We sat in his nice den, making pleasant talk with his pretty wife.

What we didn't know was that he had been busted by the police that afternoon. As we sat there, they were offering immunity if he would help them nab somebody bigger than he.

So, he dumped on us big time. As we sat there waiting for him, he phoned home and his little daughter answered, telling him that we were there. So, he put on a dramatic show for the detectives – tears and everything.

He told them that because he wasn't there with the drugs that he owed us, his wife and daughter were being held by us for ransom! He said we were the meanest and most powerful local big shots in the Brotherhood. He pleaded with the cops to rescue his beloved family.

Well, it was all baloney.

But the cops wanted us.

Within minutes, his house was surrounded by police – everybody from the California Highway Patrol to the local sheriff, the small-town police chief, four or five security guards from the housing complex's main gate and probably even a Fish and Wildlife Department game warden or two with tranquilizer guns.

TV and newspaper reporters swarmed in, filming the "stand-off" – cops over megaphones behind riot shields telling us to release our hostages and come out with our hands up.

It was night and lights shone blindingly into the house from all directions, so that we couldn't see anything.

We saw it would be suicide to try to shoot our way out. So we decided to split up rather than wait for them to come in after us. We ran three different ways. The police saw us and started shooting. As I ran, I could hear bullets pinging all around me.

I was caught and sent to the Visalia County jail. We were charged with armed abduction for ransom. The story of our attempted "kidnap" filled the front pages of the newspapers. We knew we had been framed.

The charge was bogus.

I had been in custody for two weeks when it all began to fit together, though. Two homicide detectives from Los Angeles came to see me.

"Are you Blajos, known as Conejo?" they demanded.

"I'm Art Blajos," I replied.

"We're charging you with first-degree murder for hire. We have two eyewitnesses."

I was furious. I had not committed this particular crime they were describing. They had put these supposed "witnesses" up to this. It was a total frame-up!

"You must be crazy!" I said. "Why are you doing this to me?"

They knew what they were doing. They intended to get me off the streets permanently.

I had been convicted previously of four other felonies. If I was found guilty of the kidnap charges, I would officially be labeled a Habitual Criminal, which meant that I would probably be imprisoned for the rest of my life.

But in addition to the kidnap charge there was this murder charge. Murder is a capital offense.

If found guilty, I would face the death penalty.

Then the formal charges came down.

I was facing nineteen counts – all felonies. A conviction on any one of them could put me back into the slammer for life.

The authorities were serious about shutting me down. From free-spending party guy and drug dealer, I went to facing very probably life imprisonment and possible execution.

While I was at Visalia County Jail, Irene became a regular visitor, bringing me money and drugs and acting as my runner on the outside.

Then, one day, she asked me to marry her.

I thought she had gone crazy! She told me she liked my style, but romance aside, we could be good for each other. I told her I would think about it overnight and give her an answer the next day.

I knew that for Irene, getting married to me would be a smart career move. She enjoyed the trappings of the Brotherhood lifestyle – I could tell that she had fallen as much for the image as for the man. Also my name would give her respect and authority.

And with my connections, she would be able to make money for us on the outside. As for me, I was facing at best life imprisonment, and at worst the death penalty.

So, marriage couldn't be any worse than that!

Through Irene I would have a steady supply of money and drugs, and having a wife would look good on my record in court. It would also guarantee me conjugal visits – quiet privacy with my wife. That meant a lot.

I stood to gain a great deal by marrying Irene and nothing to lose. So the next day I agreed to the marriage. Two weeks later, before a Catholic priest and with a prison guard as my best man, I said "I do."

There was a strange sort of appropriateness about it all, since I had been raised by the prison system and had spent more than half of my life in the prison system.

Now here in my thirties, I was getting married in prison! The ceremony didn't move me emotionally. Our wedding was basically the formalization of a business arrangement. Irene knew I didn't love her, that I had always seen her as a crime partner and a physical lover – but not as a marriage partner. She didn't go into the marriage blind.

Having seen me in action, she knew exactly the kind of man she was getting involved with.

I was transferred to Los Angeles County Jail and put on the maximum-security E Row. This was unofficially known as "Death Row," since most of the men there had been charged with capital crimes and so were fighting in court for their lives. The official death row was at San Quentin, where the men who were awaiting the death sentence were kept.

I was a realist. Ever since I had joined the Brotherhood, I had known that being caught and executed was always a possibility, so I developed a stoic attitude toward my own death.

What had happened was just an unfortunate but not entirely unexpected turn of events.

It would be accurate to say, however, that my life just was not going the way I had planned. I had intended to come out of all those years in prison an established crime figure with a guaranteed future in the underworld. Throughout it all, I expected to live honorably – at least in my own eyes.

I would never rat on any of my friends or brothers. I would work together to make life inside more bearable for my brothers.

And I would rise in the organization.

But now, it appeared that I would go back inside.

It appeared I would never come back out.

CHAPTER FIFTEEN

LIFE ON DEATH ROW

I was offered court-appointed counsel. The first lawyer they sent me walked in, looked at my notes, read the nineteen counts against me and shook his head.

"You don't need a lawyer," he said. "You need a miracle!" He walked out.

The second lawyer they offered me was a Black man. At that time, I had a very racist attitude. My gangland background had taught me to hate all Blacks.

A close friend of mine had been killed by a Black prison gang. "Get out of my face and fast!" I told the lawyer.

But I had to have a lawyer for the hearing, so the court sent me a third man. He was Black too.

I was about to dismiss him, but he looked me straight in the eye. I was struck by how green his eyes were.

He said, "My name is Albert House, and I will win this case for you!"

Something about his tone stopped me from telling him to get out. He had an air of authority, conviction and confidence.

I smirked at him.

"You're that good, huh?" I said. "You think you can get me off, do you?"

He was undeterred by my attitude. "I'm the best," he said, "and I'll beat this case for you." He seemed so sure he could do it that I found myself saying, "Okay, you're on!"

I instinctively felt it was right to go with him, but I also got Irene to check him out, just in case he was talking loud and saying nothing.

What she found astounded me.

Albert House had an awesome track record as a lawyer. My respect for his abilities as a lawyer soon developed into admiration as he represented me with great skill in court day after day. He had beaten fifty-two out of the fifty-three capital homicide cases he had fought.

I had made the right decision.

Albert began to break down the stereotypes about Black people which had built up in my mind over the years. We became very good friends.

As the months passed, he would keep telling me, "Don't worry, I'm going to beat this thing for you. All you have to do is listen to me. I know exactly what I'm doing."

He would warn me not to be a "jailhouse lawyer" – a prisoner who has an inflated opinion of his own knowledge of the law. This was good advice to me, because I had spent a lot of time in courthouses and I thought I knew a lot.

After two years in the Los Angeles County Jail, I began to get frustrated. I was under maximum security at all times, living a life of almost military discipline.

Every time I left prison for court appearances I had to face the indignity of strip searches – in which they subject you to the most degrading examination of every crevice in your body.

Two years in L.A. County felt like three years in a normal jail. Furthermore, I knew that if I was found guilty of the murder charge I would go to the Death Row at San Quentin and face the gas chamber.

So I figured that if I tried for a plea of manslaughter or second-degree murder, I might get away with a life sentence in an easier prison, where there would be the chance of escape.

I called Albert in and told him I wanted to go for a deal.

"I don't think that's a good idea," he said.

"Don't forget who's calling the shots," insisted jailhouse lawyer Art Blajos. "Either do it my way or split!"

Albert shook his head and tried to tell me what a big mistake I was making. But I was adamant, so he did as I asked. At my next court appearance I found out that he had been right.

When my motions for second-degree murder or manslaughter were brought before the judge, the two special state prosecutors who had been attached to my case wasted no time in putting their cards on the table.

"The prosecution refuses all plea bargaining by this defendant," they said. "We will not accept any motions of second-degree murder or manslaughter. The State is pushing for the death penalty."

They didn't want to just convict me – they wanted to kill me!

I turned to Albert, who shook his head.

"Now you've got no choice," he said. "You'll have to do it my way."

I had only two options: either to throw myself on the mercy of the court, which would guarantee me the death penalty, or to do things Albert's way and fight a first-degree murder conviction and hopefully beat it.

But the cards seemed stacked against me.

The State of California was determined to execute me. The District Attorney would address the juries like this:

"Ladies and gentlemen of the great State of California, you have been selected to hear evidence that will convince you beyond a shadow of a doubt that Art Blajos committed cold-blooded, premeditated murder."

He would then show them photographs of the victim, then pass around copies of my previous criminal record and those stupid psychiatric reports.

"It is your duty to return a verdict of guilty and to execute Art Blajos in the gas chamber," he continued. "Your tax dollars have paid for the gas chamber and it is your duty to rid our great State of this kind of vermin."

When I had been at San Quentin, whenever a condemned prisoner on Death Row received a visit from his family or lawyer, he would be shackled about the waist and ankles and escorted across the yard to the visiting room by two armed guards.

Another guard would stand on the rail above, rifle in hand, and would shout out, "Dead man walking!" This was a command to all the other inmates to get out of the way.

If they didn't, the guard would fire a warning shot and wait for the path to clear. The condemned man would shuffle past the other prisoners, his chains dragging on the ground, all eyes fixed on him.

I had witnessed this many times, and with mixed emotions. I had felt a sense of dread, for here was a man who was close to death. But another part of me admired him. I felt there was something heroic about him, as if he were a prisoner of war about to die at the hands of the enemy.

We would call out words of encouragement to the condemned man.

In reality these men were vicious and often insane. The chains were there as much to protect us from harm as to keep them from escaping. They might make a suicidal attack on a guard or an inmate against whom they had a grudge, hoping to get shot, not really caring because they were already condemned to death.

While I was being held on Death Row at L.A. County Jail, I had to go through this ritual. I had not yet been found guilty of murder, but the "Dead man walking" routine applied to me nonetheless.

I found that to be that man in chains myself was a very different thing to being a mere spectator. I recall the first time clearly.

I was shackled and led through the yard.

The prisoners cleared a respectful path for me.

The guard called out, "Dead man walking!"

Somehow, I was shocked to think that he was actually referring to me, or that all eyes in the yard were fixed on me. I was now one of the men I had pitied.

The State of California had complete control over me. It had raised me, fed me, housed me and clothed me since I was a mere boy. Now it was preparing to kill me.

Alone in my cell, I had no choice but to confront myself, and it wasn't easy.

So many questions about my life went through my mind – my past relationships, memories of things I had lived through, my joys and my pains.

There was no one to discuss it all with. I spent all day and all night wrestling with my thoughts. Every now and then thoughts about religion would creep into my mind.

I had seen many men die, and invariably their last words would be addressed to God. In their final moments, they would cry out to God, even if they had claimed that they didn't believe in Him. Among people who are dying, there are very few atheists.

Deep down inside, I knew there was a God, but I tried to deny it. I had lived my life in total disregard toward God and in rebellion against all authority, including God's. I had always relied on myself alone – on my own mind and will and strength and wisdom.

There had never been any room for God in my life. In fact, I knew that if there were a God, I was in big trouble. I definitely deserved to burn in hell for all eternity.

Over the years I had adopted the attitude that death was part and parcel of my way of life – it came with the territory. I just figured I would face it like a man when the time came. I had hoped that death would just be the end of me.

The lights would go out, and there would be no more Art – end of story.

But what if there was life after death? If there really was a hell, would that be my destination? That was too frightening to contemplate. The prospect of burning in an eternal pit was a big problem for me. So I insulated myself with layer upon layer of denial. I told myself that God didn't exist, and since He was mythical, then so was hell.

One day, I was called to go and see a visitor. I assumed that it would be Irene, but when I got to the visiting room, there sat a middle-aged Catholic nun wearing a black habit.

I was quite startled – even amused.

She introduced herself as Sister Helen. I told her she must have the wrong man.

"Who do you want to see?" I asked her.

"Art Blajos," she replied.

"Well, that's me. Who sent you?"

"Your family. They told me you'd recently gotten into trouble." That convinced me that she had the wrong man. I had been in prison for years.

"My family doesn't care about me," I said. "They've never sent anyone to see me in all the time I've been in prison."

Then I remembered that my cousin Eddie had recently been sent to Chino prison on a murder conviction. I suggested that she went to visit him instead.

No, she said, she was there to visit me.

At first our conversation was limited – we had absolutely nothing in common. I assumed that she was there in order to convert me, so I made it clear that she was wasting her time.

I told her she couldn't offer me anything I wanted. Despite my negative attitude, she said she would visit me again. She became my regular visitor.

She puzzled me. I could not fathom why she cared anything about me. I was not even remotely interested in studying religion.

But Sister Helen was a well-educated woman, a university teacher who had traveled all over the world. She made excellent conversation. I began to look forward to her visits as an interesting way to kill time.

I used to enjoy her stories about St Peter's Basilica in Rome and her visits to countries like Germany and Brazil. She would usually leave me with a cross or a rosary.

I would respond to her attempts to convert me with gentle teasing.

"You and I have so much in common," I said to her, only half joking. "You're willing to sacrifice your time and even your life for the faith you follow, and so am I. Basically you and I are the same, both warriors, only we're fighting on different sides of the battle."

"Arturo, you're terrible!" she cried in outrage – using my proper Spanish name. "How can you say that!"

She promised to light some candles for me and ask that a mass be said for me during her next trip to Rome.

Her reaction made me laugh.

I grew to actually like her. She was certainly the only person I ever allowed to call me Arturo!

She continued to visit me twice a month for years. She took a personal interest in me, even to the point of showing some of my drawings to the people at her university. She wanted me to develop my talent, and perhaps if I hadn't been the man I was in the environment I was in, I might have taken her up on her offers to get me involved in art courses.

She used to show my letters to the young, wayward boys at the juvenile centers she visited, to help to show them the harsh realities of life in prison.

It was after one such visit that Sister Helen came to me and remarked, "I believe that God is going to use your life, Arturo."

I couldn't believe my ears! It seemed like the most stupid statement I had ever heard in my life.

I felt like laughing in her face, but I didn't because she was my friend. I respected her.

So I stifled my laughter and told her to be cool.

I wondered if she knew she was talking to one of the most feared men in San Quentin.

If she had heard about my reputation, she apparently didn't believe it.

I told her that I was being picked on because I was Hispanic and the guards were racist. I insisted that the whole system was corrupt and biased against me, and I would ask her to light candles and pray for me.

She wasn't stupid, so she didn't believe all of my lies. But she had a lot of sympathy for me because she knew that I was living in an inhuman environment.

But there came a time when Sister Helen suddenly stopped coming to see me. I believe that a special agent took her aside and made it clear to her the kind of man she had been visiting.

Art Blajos was a dangerous, murderous man who was just using her, she was told.

She would be better off spending her time caring about some kid in Juvenile Hall, someone who was still redeemable. If that was what they did, it worked.

Sister Helen never came to see me again.

CHAPTER SIXTEEN

OUT OF JAIL, INTO DRUG ADDICTION

A fellow inmate and I decided that we would try to escape.

By this time I was at Palm Hall, a maximum security jail at Chino. No one had ever escaped from Palm Hall, so I found the whole idea a tremendous challenge.

Also, because it was unprecedented, it would be totally unexpected.

I really didn't care if I got caught trying to escape.

What did I have to lose? What did an additional five years on my prison term matter when I was already facing life imprisonment, or worse?

Over the next six months we formulated a plan and arranged for cutting tools to be smuggled in to us. The plan was to cut through the bars in our cells, which were adjacent. Then we would climb through the meshed windows on the tier, get out into the yard, climb over the barbed-wire fence, run past the gun towers and get over the main gate. A getaway car, flashing its lights as a signal, would be waiting on the road outside less than a hundred yards away from the gate.

I enlisted the aid of several brothers on my tier, and we set up an elaborate signal system from one man to another, so that my partner and I would know when a guard was coming. The brothers would create distractions and diversions, or simply turn up the volume on their TV sets and radios to drown out the noise of our sawing at the bars.

When I had first told my brothers that I was going to try to escape, they just laughed their heads off, telling me it just couldn't be done.

They said if I tried it I would get caught and put in isolation permanently.

But by the time we got near to finishing the cutting, everyone on the tier was rooting for us. The more progress we made, the closer we felt to actually getting out, and our growing confidence created an incredible energy and excitement on the whole tier. It was hard work – we had to saw day and night until our arms and backs ached, but after six months we had cut through the bars in both cells, according to plan. When the night of the escape finally came, the atmosphere was electric and the suspense was overwhelming. The night guard took a walk along the tier every two hours to check the cells. We planned to make our move as soon as the guard had completed his walk at 10 pm.

As the seconds ticked by before our time for action came, I imagined the look on the guard's face as he opened my cell the next morning and found only pillows underneath my blanket. I had even written out some notes for him, with smiley faces and messages such as, "This is what I think of your service here" and "I'm leaving because there's poor reception on Channel 4 and you never made me breakfast in bed."

I thought ahead about what I would do when I was free. I would go to Mexico first and hide out for a few months. Then I would go back to my own neighborhood and re-establish my lifestyle. The guard was almost at the end of his walk when we made our move. We squeezed through the gaps in our cell bars, but as we tried to clamber through the meshed tier windows, the guard saw a movement and ran off to get assistance. We knew there was no chance that we could get out into the yard once the alarm had been raised, so we ran back into our cells. The lights went on, and soon there were about twenty officers, fully armed with helmets, shields and guns, running their batons along the bars on our tier, cell by cell. Of course, the bars on our two cells came apart when they were tapped.

We were busted!

I had failed to escape, but over the years, my situation in the courts improved.

The juries grew tired.

Some jurors had to leave because of illness, and one of them even died.

One of the two "eye-witnesses" was himself being tried for a murder charge, so he became an unreliable witness. Finally, after four and a half years of legal fighting, the day came when the jury went out to deliberate. They were only out for a day, which is usually a bad sign.

Deep inside I was hoping against hope for the best – but expecting the worst.

I was facing a total of nineteen charges, including armed robbery and murder for hire.

As I sat waiting for the jury's decision, I prepared myself by switching off inside, shutting off my feelings. I became numb. The jury entered the courtroom and took their seats. The foreman stood to read out the verdict.

"On the charge of first-degree murder for hire we find the defendant … not guilty."

I didn't allow myself to feel relief, since there were still eighteen more counts to be heard. I could still end up with a lengthy jail sentence.

The foreman continued: "On the charge of armed robbery we find the defendant … not guilty."

And so it went on.

For each of the nineteen counts the foreman announced a "not guilty" verdict.

I had so carefully steeled myself to hear bad news that at first I couldn't take in what it all meant. I was numb.

But gradually relief set in, quickly followed by feelings of satisfaction and triumph.

It was a complete acquittal!

And there was more good news to follow. Within weeks, my

kidnap for ransom conviction was overturned on appeal because the police had denied me so many of my legal rights. Miraculously, after fighting for my life for so long, I was now a free man again.

The first thing I did after getting out of prison was to rob some big drug dealers. A beautiful French-Canadian model named Lisa knew three Italian Mafiosos in Hollywood whom I could hit for about $70,000 in one sting.

I told her to set them up, and I would take them on by myself.

That night, everything went according to plan, but I didn't have enough time to tie the three Italians up, so I had to get out of there fast!

Even before I had got to the bottom of the stairs they were leaning out over the balcony trying to get a clean shot at me, swearing up a storm.

I ran as fast as I could to the car, but I could hear them on the street behind me, so I stopped running and aimed my .38 pistol in their direction.

They all took cover, which gave me a few seconds of extra running time. By the time I reached my car I was too far away for them to hit me.

Now with money in my pocket and my reputation at an all-time high, I could afford to relax and enjoy my new freedom. I bought a house with Irene.

The Mafia became my whole world. I was willing to sacrifice everything – money, women, even freedom – for that higher purpose. But now, in the wider world outside the prisons, I saw problems. The Brotherhood had been birthed in the prisons, amidst blood and concrete and steel, and at first its members had been ruthless.

Once released from prison they had fearlessly burned every other criminal connection – we didn't care if they were Italian, Irish, Black, Jewish or even Hispanic. But the organization had a fatal weakness – drugs. Too many of our guys started sampling their own merchandise.

You just cannot do that.

I now found that many brothers were addicts. They had started as pushers, and now they were users. I thought this was pathetic and heart-breaking. I began to separate myself from them.

In my heart of hearts I was disillusioned. I wanted to get out, but that wasn't an easy thing to do. The code said "Blood in, blood out." You could only leave the organization in a pine box. I couldn't tell anyone how I was feeling – there was no one I could trust.

The Brotherhood was my life and it grieved me to see it so slack. An expression from the French philosopher Camus summed up how I felt. "To die is a little thing, but to see the meaning for your existence dissipate – this is unbearable."

Fortunately, I had Irene. She had stuck by me for nearly five years of legal maneuvering, helping me to fight for my life. And now that I was out of prison, she was willing to live with me in a loveless marriage.

But she surprised me even more when she expected companionship and emotional support. She had helped me, now it was my turn to be there for her. It irked me. She started demanding gratitude and recognition for all that she had done for me.

But I was so full of pride that I had suppressed all memory of my dependence on her while I was in prison. My attitude was that I was calling the shots now. I was in full control again. That was the way it was supposed to be, and she would just have to get used to the idea that I was back in the driver's seat. I believed that it was my destiny to beat the legal system. So she should be grateful to be involved with me at all.

"You're lucky I'm still with you," I snarled at her.

There is a wise proverb which says, "Pride goes before a fall." That ancient piece of enlightenment was to be fulfilled in my life – in a totally unexpected way. Most of the kids I grew up with had begun using heroin in their early teens. By the time they were sixteen or so, they were junkies. Few made it into their thirties unless they kicked the stuff. Out on the street, there is no such thing as an elderly junkie. The stuff destroys your liver, not to mention your mind. Even people who kick the habit begin having severe medical problems when they reach middle age — heart problems, liver malfunction, kidney complications. Heroin does a whole lot of damage and leaves a deadly legacy.

But I had stayed pretty clean — I was never interested in hard drugs, not even in my twenties. I smoked marijuana, but did not like losing control of myself. I took a few barbiturates, but that always seemed to get me in trouble with the authorities. So, I didn't have a dope-fiend mindset. I didn't get into it. I didn't long for it. I only got high once in a while, just like I got a little drunk once in a while.

But, I began to sample some of the high-quality Peruvian cocaine that I was selling. The way it started, a brother and his old lady offered me some — not to snort, but to slam or inject into your veins. It made me feel like I was Superman. *This is how I really ought to feel!* I thought. *With this stuff I can conquer the world.*

Coke made me feel that I could try anything and succeed. I felt a powerful euphoria, and yet I was also clear-headed. That was what made it so seductive. Cocaine is extremely addictive — more so than heroin, but the user feels that he is in total control. Before I knew it I was hooked.

Cocaine is a strong stimulant, and one fix would keep me high for an hour if it was quality stuff — at least in the beginning, anyway. I would lose touch with reality. So, to bring myself down, I would inject heroin, which is a sedative. Then, I could relax and end the cocaine high. I would sleep for two or three days to recuperate. Then I would feel very low, so I would start on the coke again to fight my overpowering depression.

I was addicted, but I didn't admit it.

I started taking the coke only at weekends. I thought I had it under control, but the addiction crept up on me. But when it came to completely dominate my life, I finally realized that I might have a problem. It was only when I tried to stop that I knew for sure that I was addicted. I told myself that I didn't need the coke and put what I had away. But when I tried to do all the things I used to do with the help of the coke, I found that I couldn't do them.

I had to have it.

I hated knowing that I was addicted. Jail had taught me to be a self-disciplined man, but now I knew that my will was being dominated by drugs.

The biggest danger for me was that coke made me paranoid.

I would be sitting in a room fixing with my friends. I would be on a high, but then I would start to worry that there might be special police agents from the Organized Crime Service outside, waiting to kick down the door and bust me.

"Shush! Somebody's out there!" I would whisper to the other guys.

"Naw, nobody's out there," they would say.

I would take out my gun and peer out of the window through the gap. "How do you know?" I would ask, still peering through the gap. "Or are all of you working for the cops?"

One of them would offer to go out and check for me.

"How come you want to go out there?" I would demand. "You're working for them, aren't you? This is a set up!"

By this time they would all be scared to death, their highs completely ruined by my paranoia. I would spend hours and hours worrying about the cops being outside the door. I knew there was no one out there, but what had I heard?

Not surprisingly, after a while nobody wanted to fix with me anymore, so I had to get high by myself. Of course, my paranoia was based on a real threat, because I had a lot of underworld enemies. The police didn't care much for me, either. Three times my door had been kicked in by special anti-crime agents. They put a gun to my head and raided the house, cutting mattresses open in their search for drugs. Now the cocaine in my bloodstream magnified and intensified my fear of being attacked by enemies or raided by the police.

I had become utterly miserable and desperate. The coke no longer gave me a high – it just made me paranoid – but I couldn't stop taking it. My body was dehydrated and I was wasting away, because you don't eat on coke. My addiction to cocaine and heroin was slowly but surely killing me. I was losing my mind.

I felt that I was going to die soon. I was taking some incredible risks. One time I took on eight men and robbed them of their drugs at gun point! I figured that if they attacked me, I would at least take down two or three of them with me. I had developed a high tolerance to the drugs, so I needed to take more and more to get any effect. Even normal junkies would warn me about taking so much. They weren't really so concerned about me – they just didn't want to be around when I finally overdosed and died, because of my status in the Brotherhood. They were afraid that they would be blamed for my death.

The addiction began to get me into trouble with my contacts in the drugs business. I would forget where I had put packets of coke worth thousands of dollars each. I would forget to make payments.

Also my relationship with Irene began to fall apart. We were living in the same house, but we were not living together. I began to play around with other women.

She would say, "You're so cold! I waited for you while you were in jail, I worked hard as your runner, and now you're with other women!"

"I'm just making up for lost time," I would reply.

The truth was, I wasn't really capable of loving anyone – not even Irene. She had been faithful to me throughout my time on

Death Row. Now I was treating her with such ingratitude. Not surprisingly, she began to hate me. I would tell her, the Brotherhood comes first with me – I had told her that when we got married, and it was still true. Nothing had changed. So she could either flow with that or hit the road!

She began seeing other men.

It didn't bother me much, because I didn't really think of her as my wife any longer. But I warned her that if I caught her with another man in our house, I would kill them both. She knew I meant it.

"You're not the man I used to know!" she would say. "You're a junkie. You used to be a strong man, and I respected you for it. But now you're weak!"

I would tell her, "I'm in control of myself! I'm not strung out. I made you and everything you've got. I can take it all away again if I want!"

In my heart I knew she was right – I was totally controlled by my addiction. So I told her I was going to stay in for three or four days and kick the addiction. She just laughed in disbelief. But I was as good as my word, and over the next few days I went through the withdrawals.

On the second night I was lying on the floor, shaking and sweating, and a television evangelist was speaking. I didn't like preachers, but there was something about this one that made me listen.

He pointed at the camera, and it seemed as if pointing directly at me. "You, right there on the floor, going through drug withdrawal – Jesus died to save you!" he said. "You're sick and tired of being hooked on drugs. Jesus can change your life. Tonight he can set you free!"

I felt as if an electric shock had gone through me. *What was that?* I thought. *That was weird!*

I changed TV channels and got up and walked back and forth, wondering what it meant. I thought I was losing my mind. All I could think about was that preacher's finger pointing at me. To take my mind off it, I went out and robbed a drug dealer!

So, I was taking cocaine again.

Irene, gave up on me and filed for a divorce. I was only surprised it had taken her so long to get around to it! I told her to take the house – I didn't care. I was hopelessly addicted and had stopped caring about anything except getting my fix.

After Irene and I split up, I lived with one set of friends after another. They didn't actually want me in their homes, but they were afraid of me, so they let me stay a couple of days. I wasn't a very pleasant guest! Sometimes I would freak out and get paranoid. I would imagine I had heard a voice, and would kick doors down in a panic.

I kept on the move all the time, drifting from house to house. Every day I had to get money for my fix, so I would rob stores and drug dealers. I was taking a lot of risks.

The biggest worry to me was the Brotherhood itself. I had become a threat to them. I was losing my grip, and I knew too much about them. They would send guys around to warn me. I would assure them that the money was on its way, that everything was taken care of.

As the visits became more frequent, I began to get angry.

"Get out of my face!" I would tell them. "My word is good! Don't come around here any more. I'll be in touch with you."

It was getting very dangerous for me. I knew it.

But I was still a high-ranking member of the organization. I still had reputation and respect. They didn't have enough against me to warrant a hit. They just figured that I was having a rough time and that I would shape up again.

But I knew that my time was running out. It was just a matter of time before somebody decided I was a liability.

It was just a matter of time before I got a bullet in the head from the Mafia or the police.

Maybe I would die of an overdose first. In my heart I knew that my nine lives were all used up. The sand in my hourglass was almost all gone.

I went to a church to make things right with God. It was a big, traditional cathedral.

I had gotten myself shot doing business, but the wound wasn't that serious. I thought maybe in the church, I would hear God's voice or have a miracle or something. I was fighting drug withdrawal. I was in torment. I wanted peace. There was no one I could talk to. I had never imagined I would end up like this. I was totally alone. I had lost my wife, my home, the respect of my peers, everything. The loneliness was overwhelming.

So I walked into the big, empty church. There were candles everywhere. I went up to the baptistery and figured that was where they probably kept the Holy Water, like in the movie *The Exorcist*, which was about a girl who was demon possessed.

I splashed some water on my face.

Nothing happened. I honestly thought that maybe it would burn or knock me out or maybe that something evil in me would react to it.

But nothing happened – no demons jumped out of me!

I walked outside, disappointed.

I stayed for a while with a drug dealer named Susan who lived in Hollywood. One day I overdosed on cocaine and collapsed on the floor.

She was horrified. She thought I was going to die. But I knew that I had to stay awake. If I fell asleep, I would never wake up. So I got up off the floor. Then I collapsed, but got up again. This happened three or four times.

Susan was about to call an ambulance, not caring that she would get busted for drug possession. She put ice on my head.

She slapped me around the face until I was black and blue.

She made me walk around the apartment, until she was sure I was going to be all right. She had seen a lot of people overdose, but she had never seen someone take as much as I had taken and get up and survive.

But I had not lost my will to live. I did not die. Instead, I did kick cocaine. However, I did it by getting deeper and deeper into heroin.

Many times in my life I had sensed death. Sometimes I had almost tasted or smelled the presence of impending death around some men.

A day or two later they would die.

That same sense of impending death was all around me.

CHAPTER SEVENTEEN

A DATE WITH THE EXECUTIONER

Then I was arrested for drunk-driving.

The police found the heroin tracks on my arm, so I was sent to the county jail for sixty days – to kick my addiction.

I desperately wanted to get free. I had dreams about starting a new life in Arizona and never looking back. Two months in jail was a good opportunity to make it happen.

But there was this complication – Eddie Guzman.

He was on the hit list. He had been missing, on the run. Now, I had found him – right there in the cell next to mine. I was obligated to take the Brotherhood's ultimate revenge.

I had to kill him.

Within hours of my arrival, I had gotten a homemade knife passed to me for the purpose at hand. I knew the showers would be the best time to kill him. But I had to gain his trust. There in my cell, as I was going cold turkey off heroin, I started talking with him about his Bible. I passed hours with him, listening to his religious babble, then telling him lies about Irene and other women.

As my withdrawal intensified, I paced up and down in my cell, smoking cigarettes, trying to tough-out the pain, talking with Eddie, gaining his trust like a cobra seduces a mouse. In my paranoia, it seemed that everybody in the cell block was waiting, watching, knowing what was going down.

Then there was the night that he called my name. "Hey, Conejo, look over here."

And there was Eddie sitting up with a tourniquet on his arm, injecting cocaine. "You know what, Conejo?" he said as he shot up. "Jesus Christ can change your life."

I don't know if you can truly understand how very mad his words made me. With a needle in his vein, such religious talk was sacrilege. He was shooting in front of me while I was hurting and he was mocking me by coming across like some holy mother of mercy. It turned my stomach.

But I hid my intense anger and answered him, "Hey, homeboy, tell me about Jesus."

And, stoned that he was, he did.

And that night, he left that Bible of his in the bars.

And I read it in the stillness of the wee morning hours.

I woke up to the sound of knocking on the bars of my cell. A food tray was being pushed under the bars. I had been asleep for hours. I checked to make sure that the Bible was out of sight – good, it was hidden under my blanket. Then it sudenly dawned on me – I had been asleep! How could that be? When you're going through withdrawal you don't sleep – not for at least ten days. And I felt hungry too, so I started to eat. But that was impossible – I should have been unable to eat because of stomach cramps. As I ate the food and drank the coffee, I felt good.

I felt great!

"Are you coming out?" asked the guard.

In the next cell, Eddie was coming out for his shower.

I reached for my knife. A bunch of other guys were walking down the ramp. My opportunity was there. Everybody knew what was coming down. A lot of guys pushed into the shower. They would cover for me. Soon Eddie would be a corpse testifying to the folly of doublecrossing the Brotherhood.

I stepped outside. Eddie walked just ahead of me.

He draped his towel over his shoulders.

I caught knowing glances from the other inmates. They were going to see his blood flow.

I walked down the corridor. I held my blade under my towel

– out of sight. Eddie suspected nothing. He had been completely reassured by our conversations.

Whenever I was about to strike a victim, I made sure that I never looked in their eyes. I would look only at where I was going to thrust the blade.

The moment was coming.

The guard stepped away.

Steam rose from the shower room. Eddie put his head back under a stream of water. I began to whirl around and strike him in the heart, but then I looked at his eyes.

When I did, I felt something hit me like a wave. Somehow I saw Eddie as a human being – as a person, a father, a husband, a son – not just a target.

He was *alive*.

I was going to *end* it all for him – something he did not deserve.

Such second thoughts had never bothered me before. I had always been able to switch off my emotions and just take care of business.

Eddie stared at me.

He knew what was happening.

He stared at me, transfixed, like a terrified little mouse. He did not resist. In the next seconds, he would be dead, his face in the drain. Everyone would step out as if nothing had happened. They would return to their cells as I mixed in with them. The knife would disappear. Nobody would be blamed for the dead man in the shower.

It was time for the blood.

It was time.

But I did not move.

If I did not kill him, I would have to answer to the Brotherhood. This would probably be the last straw. I had showed weakness. I had shamed the Brotherhood.

I clutched the knife.

I stared into Eddie's terrified eyes.

I did not strike him. It was not something dramatic, such as that I realized I had no right to play God. No, I just didn't want to hurt him.

I walked out of the shower, trembling.

Why did I let him get to me? I mumbled to myself. *He should be dead by now!* I knew I wasn't scared of him. He wasn't even armed – he was stark naked. It should have been simple.

He brushed past me and returned to his cell.

And I didn't kill him. That was the first time in my fifteen-year career as an assassin that I'd had a target within striking distance and had let him go.

It depressed me.

I went back to my cell without taking a shower.

How could I have let this happen?

But Eddie was happy, convinced that I was his friend. He knew I'd had the chance to kill him – but didn't do it. He told me I could keep his Bible.

I placed it on the bars of his cell.

He smiled at me and handed me a pack of cigarettes. I took them since I was running out.

I had never expected this turn of events. I was scared that I was losing my mind.

I had to get it together! In my cell, I washed up a little and shaved and did some pushups.

I told myself that this wasn't the end of the world. Eddie was still within striking distance. I had the remainder of my sixty days to get him.

I had a further advantage now that he believed we were friends.

But what really scared me was that now *I just didn't want to kill him*.

Eddie and I continued talking during the days that followed. He told me a lot more about Jesus and the Bible. He told me about the strong men like Joshua and Samson.

"Samson was a really bad dude," he said. "He killed hundreds of guys."

I was impressed by characters like that. I liked tough, warrior figures. I had always modeled myself on the strong men of history.

So he would pass me his Bible and I read more and more of it. What interested me about Samson and Joshua and Moses and Jeremiah was that these men all seemed to draw their power from the same source – God. As I read the Bible, it began to change me, although I didn't realize it.

The other prisoners were surprised that I was reading a Bible. They were even more baffled that Eddie wasn't dead.

However, no one dared to ask any questions or to ridicule me by suggesting that I had gone soft. I was still feared and respected.

I was still secure in my identity as a Mafia member.

I wasn't afraid of talking about the Bible and asking questions about Jesus. This was nothing unusual in the prison culture: men would often discuss religion.

I began having intense, violent dreams at night. In these dreams I did superhuman deeds, things I had always wanted to do. I would wake up feeling violent, but when I read the Bible I would find a sense of peace.

I had totally kicked my heroin habit – without all the pain and sleeplessness. This was unheard of – it should have been much harder and taken much longer.

I was gaining weight and feeling healthy.

I had studied the power of the mind and had read books about Eastern philosophy, and so I just assumed that my success in kicking the addiction was a case of mind over matter.

Amazingly, as word got around that I was reading the Bible, some of the other prisoners started asking me religious advice! One guy named Juan came to me while I was in my cell and told me he was angry because he suspected that his wife was having an affair with another man. He was wearing a crucifix around his neck.

I looked at him and said, "Juan, you see that thing around your neck? Do you believe in that?"

This stunned him. "Well, I guess so," he said.

"So why don't you pray?" I suggested. "If you believe in Him, talk to Him."

"Do you think it'll work?"

"I don't know, but why not try it?" I didn't really know what I was talking about. I knew I was out of my depth.

I was mystified about what was going on.

There was no reaction from the Mafia to my failure to kill Eddie.

I got word that they understood that sometimes circumstances weren't right and it was wiser to wait for the right opportunity. Somehow, word did not get out that I had been within striking distance and I had let him get away.

If it had, they wouldn't have been so tolerant.

Eddie continued using drugs, but the fact that I had kicked the habit impressed him. He decided to follow suit. His girlfriend had been smuggling in drugs for him, but he decided he didn't want to put her at risk any more.

One night I was thinking about the life of the Apostle Paul and all that he had suffered for his switch of allegiance. He had been a hit man for the enemies of the Christians. Then, all of a sudden, he was a missionary, preaching all about God to foreigners. A verse in Acts said about Paul, "I will show him how much he must suffer for my name," (Acts 9:18).

I was impressed by the way the early followers of Jesus had been so committed to Him and had been willing to suffer for Him. As a Mafia member, I knew what it was like to be committed to a cause.

If I was going to suffer, I wanted it to be for a worthwhile cause.

I started wondering if Jesus was real, if He really was who He said He was. Without quite realizing that I was talking to anybody in particular, I said, "I would be willing to suffer for

You too – for Your name."

I laid on my bunk and stared at the ceiling of my cell.

Suffering for good made sense.

Suffering for evil – as I had all my life – suddenly seemed absurd.

I knew that I couldn't continue to be a member of the Brotherhood.

I had this compelling desire to serve Jesus – just like this former killer, Paul, had.

Yet there was no way out of the Brotherhood except death.

So I asked the Lord to somehow enable me to escape from the Brotherhood so that I could serve Jesus. I felt that if there really was a God who was mighty enough to free me from the life I had led, I surely would be willing to suffer for Him.

Then I read this passage in Acts, where God was speaking to Paul in a vision: "Do not be afraid, keep on speaking, do not be silent. For I am with you, and no one is going to attack or harm you, because I have many people in this city." I felt that somehow God was going to do the same for me.

What I was reading in the Bible convinced me that God was real, and that what He said He would do, He had the power to do. Jesus had said that He could change my life and erase my sins. I knew precisely the kind of man I was: a hunter of men, consumed with my own pleasures, cold to the needs of anyone else. It was very hard for me to imagine that God could really love someone like me, but I was beginning to believe it.

My sixty days were almost up, and I never got around to killing Eddie.

He suggested that I should go and see a guy named Joe Lugo, whom we had both known at San Quentin. Eddie said he was now working with an organization called Victory Outreach. I had never heard of them.

I went straight there.

That in itself was a miracle. Normally after being released

from jail I would go to a friend's house to score some drugs and a girl. I walked the two miles from the county jail to the Victory Outreach church.

Only, it wasn't a fancy place like the cathedral where I had gone in search of Holy Water.

It was an ordinary-looking house. A guy was sweeping the asphalt outside.

"Are you looking for Victory Outreach?" he asked me. "It's that house there," he said with a happy smile.

I knocked on the door, and Joe Lugo, the Home Director, came out. He was amazed when he saw me.

"Conejo? What are you doing here?"

I told him that Eddie had suggested that I go to see him.

Joe didn't know what to do with me. I could tell he was wondering if I had been sent by the Brotherhood to kill him.

A little guy called Joseph came up behind him. Joe told him to take me into the back room and pray for me.

"Come on, sinner," said Joseph.

I wasn't sure how to take that – was it some kind of compliment? In junior high, that was what we had called our street gang. Joseph led me into a little wooden office at the back of the house. As we stood there, he started telling me how to become a Christian. He kept calling me a sinner, which I was getting tired of.

Then he told me he was going to pray for me.

"Put your hands up," he said.

"What?"

"Put your hands up," he insisted.

"Are you the police?" I snapped at him. "Only the police tell me to put my hands up!"

"That's how to pray," Joseph said. "Pray with your hands up, like you're surrendering to the Holy Spirit."

I thought he was nuts and was beginning to feel stupid. If anyone had walked into that office right then, I would have stormed out.

"Close your eyes," he told me.

"No way!" I said.

"Repeat after me." He started praying: "Lord Jesus…"

He waited for me to repeat it.

"Just what do you think you're doing?" I demanded.

"I'm praying for you. You're a sinner, and I'm going to lead you to Jesus."

This little guy was completely fearless! People just didn't talk to me like that! But something made me want to go along with him.

He began praying again: "Lord Jesus…"

"Come into my heart."

I said it, still thinking this guy was nuts: "Come into my heart."

"I believe you're the Son of God," led Joseph. "forgive me for my sins."

I repeated these words, and all of a sudden I noticed raindrops falling on the carpet. I looked up – there was a roof over our heads, so how could it be raining in here?

Then I realized that the raindrops were actually my own tears!

I had not cried in many years; I couldn't remember the last time I had wept.

I felt stupid and wanted to run away. But I knew that something was happening. Right there in that humble little room, in front of this obnoxious little guy Jesus Christ came into my heart.

I believed!

I stood there weeping for quite a long time.

"That's the Lord, that's the Lord," said Joseph in a matter-of-fact voice.

I felt as if a blast of fresh air had just hit me. I could breathe freely. A weight and a tension had come off me and something living had come into me. In the few seconds it took me to pray that simple prayer, the power of God came into my heart and renewed me.

In that short time Jesus Christ did for me what seventeen years of prison, psychiatrists, lawyers, drugs, money, power and sex had been unable to do. He had given me a new heart! The realization came upon me that God really had saved me from my sins – just like I had read about in the county jail.

It was a cleansing feeling.

A tremendous load had been taken off my shoulders. I felt a release, a freedom, a peace and a joy I had never known before. I was amazed at the things I had been reading about in Eddie's borrowed Bible really were true, and that I had actually met God personally. I was overwhelmed with a sense of the presence of Jesus. I knew that a dramatic change had taken place in my life. Joseph rushed out and told Joe Lugo what had happened.

Joe was overjoyed.

"Conejo!" he cried, "you've given your life to Jesus! Praise God!"

Gone was the fear in his eyes. Joe embraced me as a brother. "I've been praying for you for a long time!" he told me.

"You're kidding, *ese!*"

"No way! I kept having this vision of you before my eyes that I didn't understand. I was supposed to pray for you, I guessed. I didn't know what else it could be, unless maybe it was a warning –." He squinted at me, somewhat embarrassed.

But I understood.

He'd had every right to be scared of what crazy thing I might do. As I stood there with tears streaming from my eyes, and I felt no shame or embarrassment. Only joy.

My conversion that day was the greatest moment of my life. I now understood who Jesus really was: *the Christ, the Son of the Living God.* And I also understood who and what I really was: *a wretched sinner.* It was a great miracle – Jesus had come to live in me, to give me a new life. In the Bible, God makes this promise: "I will give you a new heart and put a new spirit in you; I will remove from you your heart of stone and give you a heart of flesh" (Ezekiel 36:26).

That promise has been fulfilled in my life.

God had interrupted my miserable existence and given me a second chance.

CHAPTER EIGHTEEN

BE FOR REAL

Now, I truly was a walking dead man.

The Brotherhood would find out.

Joe invited me to stay there at the Victory Outreach Home. It turned out that this was no ordinary church. Loosely affiliated with one of the largest denominations in the world, Victory Outreach is actually more than 500 churches and rehabilitation homes all over the world.

Each house is filled with men or women like me, recovering alcoholics and former addicts – usually with sordid histories of prostitution, armed robbery, prison time, murder ... you name it.

These rehabs are generally located in the very worst sections of the most violent neighborhoods of America's biggest cities – but also in places like London, Amsterdam, Mexico City, San Salvadore, Barcelona, Caracas, Santiago and São Paulo. There is a joke that when the drive-by shootings and drug sales and sidewalk prostitutes get so bad that a traditional church packs up and moves to the safe suburbs, then you can expect Victory Outreach to show up.

That is exactly what has happened all over the world. Former rejects of society catch the vision of Victory Outreach founder Sonny Arguinzoni – himself a former heroin addict rescued off the streets of Brooklyn in the early 1960s under the street outreach of Teen Challenge, then led by former small-town pastor David Wilkerson and ex-gang warlord Nicky Cruz.

The pastor of Victory Outreach church was Nolberto Gomez

who himself came from a life of crime and drugs.

So, I moved in.

There I was baptized – dunked under. The water did not burn my face. But I was filled with immense joy all over again.

"Brother, you need to spend some time here," Joe said as I toweled off. "You need to learn about what has just happened to you. People like us, we're messed up inside, and we need to give God a chance to sort us out. You need to place yourself in His hands."

I wasn't so sure.

"Brother, you won't be able to make it in any other church," said Joe. "They wouldn't know how to handle you."

Well, he had a point there.

And the prospect of trying to make it back in the world I had come from was just a little scary, too. None of my friends were going to understand when I didn't want to get high or go rob a convenience grocery store.

Nolberto told me I had become a new creation when I gave my life to Jesus. "You're brand new. You've got to take some time to learn who you have become. You have a new identity. You need to stay here at the home for your own protection.'

"What do you mean by that?" I asked.

"You belong to God now, so the devil wants to kill you. You're probably at the top of his hit-list, because you used to belong to him in a big way, and he used you. Now God is going to use you, and the devil doesn't want that to happen. God wants you to go out and tell people about Jesus."

I grinned.

"You think I'm going to turn into a preacher?"

Pastor Nolberto smiled. "You need to stay here at the home. It isn't going to be easy for you. You're used to being the boss, to calling the shots. We don't have a lot of money here. All you'll get here is beans and rice to eat, but you'll hear all you need to hear about Jesus Christ."

You see, there is not a lot of money in inner-city,

rehabilitation-type work. A lot of people donate a lot of money to foreign missionaries and all sorts of causes, such as saving baby seals and protecting whales. However, giving money to rehabilitate druggies and hookers and thieves is not as glamorous.

Some people would rather not think that America has those kind of problems.

They really don't care to get involved.

So, I got a crash course in depending on God. People constantly said, "The Lord will provide."

Well, guess what? He does. It can be downright amazing.

"Ok," I said. "I'll stay here."

Joe told me, "You've got to give God time to speak into your life. You're here to get to know God. And you will get your calling to serve God. Who knows? You may even end up being a pastor. Quite a few men who have passed through here are now leading churches."

He named a few ex-gangsters whom I knew, and I found it hard to believe that they were now preaching after living the way they had lived. Joe pulled out some press clippings and showed me their names in print.

I was amazed. "They must have been changed by God," I said.

"Yes," said Joe, "and that's what's happened to you too, only you don't realize it yet."

He went on to tell me about the outreach's vision of "treasures out of darkness", of bringing people from the streets to know Jesus as their Saviour and Lord, rescuing them from drugs, crime and violence and leading them to serve Jesus with their lives.

I spent eleven months at the men's home there. There were about a dozen other men staying at the home at that time, and Joe introduced them all to me. They looked like losers and drug addicts.

But I was not the one to judge!

Sure, I had been conditioned by my gangster lifestyle to despise anyone who was weak. A couple of these guys knew me, and at first they found it hard to believe that I had really become a Christian. I looked like a scam – maybe I was hiding from the cops or else trying to hit somebody who was on the run from the Brotherhood. They were obviously afraid of me, and it took several of them a while to trust me. Some of them admitted later to secretly hoping that I wasn't going to stay in the home!

Later that first day, I walked outside and there was a beautiful blue sky. It was as if it was the first time I had seen such a thing – previously I had never really noticed the sky. And in the garden there was an almond tree in bloom, with white blossoms. I could smell the delicious fragrance. I looked at this tree for a long time. And I studied the other trees, and the grass – everything seemed different now.

It was a time of wonder for me. Now I could see the good things about people. I could talk to them naturally and enjoy their company.

My defenses had come down. I was no longer looking for people's weaknesses in case I needed to fight them or destroy them. I no longer felt I had to be sure of my escape routes, constantly thinking about my next move, calculating how I was going to handle this or that situation.

My cynical mind-set was changing.

Later that day I sat in on my first Bible study. It was a strange sight, because these guys didn't look like normal Christians. In fact, they all looked as if they belonged in the yard at San Quentin! They were reading the first chapter of John's Gospel. The guy who was doing the teaching had a big mustache and lots of tattoos, and his English was rough. He kept slipping in and out of street slang.

Then there was a time of worship, which seemed weird to me. Everybody stood up, so I stood up.

They sang and clapped their hands a lot.

I just stood there in amazement, watching all this strange

behavior. And I looked at Joe, wondering what was happening. But he was caught up in the worship as well.

He was praying out loud, "Thank you, Lord, for saving Art! Thank you for making him our brother!"

I knew deep within me that word was somehow spreading. The Brotherhood knew that Eddie was still alive. They would learn all too soon that I was missing — and hooked up with a bunch of religious fanatics.

Believe me, that's exactly what they were.

They were enthusiastic. They were devoted to God. And they gave Him the same fervor that friends of mine gave to the Raiders football team on TV or to Lakers basketball. I had never seen anything like it. Plus, my conversion was a real miracle to them. They declared that it was a powerful testimony to God's ability to save people from sin and bondage, and so, they were all giving thanks and praise to God for what he had done in my life.

But I felt rather embarrassed by all of it.

I just hoped the service would all be over soon.

Then Joe said to me, "Conejo, we want to pray for you."

"OK," I said. "Go for it."

"I'm going to lay my hands on you — that's how we pray for people. I want to pray a blessing on you."

So they all gathered around me and put their hands on my shoulders and my head and my arms. With his eyes closed, Joe prayed, "Jesus, please protect Art and surround him with your mighty warrior angels!"

Loudly, all the people around me bound the power of the devil in my life.

"Satan!" yelled one former burglar and crack addict, "you have had control of this man's life. Now your time is up! Art now belongs to Jesus!"

I was thinking to myself, what on Earth is going on? What are they all talking about? I started having some doubts about the decision I had taken. I was wondering if I had gotten myself involved with a bunch of nuts! I felt very awkward. I had to get alone and talk to God.

I looked up at Joe, hoping he could help me understand what this was all about, but he was praying passionately to Jesus, thanking him for converting me, tears welling up in his eyes.

Somehow, God gave me the grace to just stand there while they prayed for me. Eventually they finished, and I backed off so that they couldn't go at it again!

That night I stayed at the home, sharing a small room with several other guys.

Previously I wouldn't have been willing to do that – they weren't in the same league as me. But my attitude was different. They were Christians and now I was one too, and we somehow had something in common – even if they did look like no-ambition low-lifes. They were very kind and friendly to me and did their best to make me feel at home. They even let me have the best bed in the room.

As I lay there in the darkness beside the window, I heard something approach my bed.

It was making the sort of huffing and snorting noises that a horse makes, but its footfalls were like those of a man. The other guys were fast asleep, so only I heard this.

I felt afraid and very cold.

I knew there was something there beside my bed, so I started thinking about finding a gun or a knife. That was my usual response when faced with danger – but there were no weapons at hand. I became paralyzed with fear.

I couldn't even speak.

I feared that if I were to look up, I would be looking right at whatever it was, standing beside the window.

But then I remembered the last thing the guys in the room had been talking about before they fell asleep. One of them had mentioned Jehovah, one of the Old Testament names for God.

First, I thought the name "Jehovah" in my mind.

Then I was able to speak out his name: "Jehovah!"

And then I was able to sit up in bed.

There was nothing there by the window.

I went outside the house – but there was nothing out there either.

But I knew that something evil had been next to my bed. I later found out that many newly converted Christians have experiences like this – where they are attacked by irrational fear.

The following morning there was a prayer time at an extremely early hour. I didn't much like having to get up so early, but I went along with it. They read a few passages from the Book of Proverbs about wisdom. I understood it well enough and was encouraged by it, but I wasn't too pleased when they started singing again.

They sang worship songs to Jesus, telling him how glad they were He had set them free – and all this at 5.30 in the morning!

Then they sat down or knelt down and spent time praying right out loud, asking God to save their families and friends. I sat down too, feeling very self-conscious.

I thought it was all crazy.

Occasionally someone would pray for me. I would feel embarrassed.

This went on for about an hour. It seemed a very long time to me before we had breakfast!

Over bacon and eggs, Joe and I talked. He could tell I was having a little trouble with all the Pentecostalism. What little church I had ever known had been formal Catholicism. This loud singing and emotional praying was totally foreign to me. Even at the boys' home, Sister Barbara had prayed for me – but it had been quiet and meditative.

And respectful.

This was respectful, too – but, well, I was having some problems.

Joe tried to encourage me. "Conejo, you're a new creation now," he said. "You used to make a stand in public for the Brotherhood, but now you've got to do it for Jesus. Don't be embarrassed. Remember that the people you're now talking to about Jesus are the same people who have feared and respected you. They will still respect you now – they will listen to what you say to them. But you've got to be real with them. You can't do stuff just because everybody else here is doing it."

He was right.

It had to be real or I wasn't going to stick around.

I'd been conned quite enough in my life.

I wasn't going to con myself into a fake religion. I chose reality.

This was not the kind of Christianity I had encountered in jail. I had covered my head with my pillow when Christians had visited, playing their guitars and banging their tambourines. This was real, down-to-earth Christianity. I saw it had the power to change the lives of people like me.

I realized I had to become willing to go out into the real world and talk to real people who were bound by real sin and real oppression and bring them the message of Jesus Christ.

So, in the weeks to come, I did.

And word spread.

Friends would call on me at the home, and would be greatly puzzled. "What are you doing here with these people, Conejo? You don't belong here with these crazies!"

"I've become a Christian," I would tell them.

Quite often the guys from the rehab went out into really dangerous neighborhoods and preached on bullhorns. We played loud Christian music and talked with people – and sometimes even put on plays. The term we used was "blasting." Some even called it a "spiritual drive-by" as in a street-gang drive-by shooting.

So, here I would be, passing out Christian tracts. I would see somebody I had known from prison. They would give me a blank look, not knowing what to say.

"So you're going to be staying here, in that place, with these people?" they would ask in disbelief.

"That's right. If you want to find me, this is where I'll be."

They would leave shaking their heads, thinking it was a shame that their friend Conejo had gone crazy.

My wife, Irene, heard rumors, so she came to the home to check it out for herself. Our divorce was almost final, but she still cared about me.

"What is the matter with you?" she demanded.

I told her. "I've become a Christian."

She didn't believe me. "I know you," she said. "You can't fool me!"

"But it's true!" I protested.

"You're the coldest, most vicious man I've ever known," she reminded me, "and you're a liar! You're working an angle. You will never really change!"

"I've been born again," I said. "I'm a new man now."

A tear rolled down my face.

That really blew her mind. The Art she used to know had never wept.

"All that coke must have really messed you up," was the only explanation she could think of.

"Look at me," I told her.

"I see you," she said.

And she walked away.

The men staying at the home had to work at a nearby car wash to generate income for the home and to learn the work ethic. One day I was working when a big Cadillac came and parked alongside the car wash.

I felt a sudden warning deep within me.

Well, this would be it.

I had been living on borrowed time anyway.

I found myself strangely unprepared to die. I knew I was about to be killed, but it wasn't right. I wasn't at peace about going up to heaven and being with God and the angels for ever and ever. No, I had this feeling that I wasn't supposed to go yet.

I had work to do.

What kind of work? Washing cars?

No – something else.

I looked at the Cadillac. I had no idea who was inside. I waited. Nothing happened. I kept washing cars. Guys around me were singing Christian choruses – and they were very poor singers. It was less than inspirational!

Nothing about it was dramatic.

I hadn't expected it to be this way. I had always figured that when I died I would go out in a blaze of glory, in a fight with a gun or a knife in my hand. I had never expected to be gunned down while holding two wet rags and listening to a couple of recovering crack addicts try to sing! This was pitiful and humiliating!

The power window rolled down.

I calmly stepped over to the Caddie.

I was asked one question: "What's happening?"

My life depended on my answer, because what they were really asking was, "Tell us we've heard wrong."

I was tempted to lie to these guys, to tell them that really I was using the home as a front to impress the police and my parole officers, and what better scam than this? I wanted to tell them, "I'm still me, nothing has changed. Be cool."

But I found that I couldn't lie.

I couldn't deny what had happened to me that day when I had asked Jesus to come into my life.

I stood there, watching them wait for my answer. My heart was hammering and my mind was in a whirl. These were the people I had fought and killed for – for whom I had almost died.

I had spent years of my life in prison for them.

And now they were threatening me with death while I stood holding two wet rags.

I whispered this prayer: "Lord Jesus, if you're real, get busy!"

At that moment I made a decision in my heart. I gave them my answer: "I'm serving the Lord now. I'm a Christian."

They just sat there looking at each other, probably wondering if they had heard me correctly. They looked at me again, and I stood there waiting for them to blow my head off. I could imagine my brains being splattered all over the car wash asphalt. I could almost smell that familiar scent of gunsmoke.

But nothing happened.

There was a long, awkward silence.

I just stood there, feeling stupid and helpless.

But I felt something else too – a presence which seemed to be making them nervous!

And then they just drove off. I watched them go. I could breathe again.

About a week later I had another visit.

This time, the message was this: "Be for real."

That was a Brotherhood motto. They were saying, "You've made your decision. Don't turn back."

I now know that the message really came from God.

CHAPTER NINETEEN

FACING CHOICES

There were some aspects of being a Christian which I found very hard to accept, especially the need to submit to the leaders of the church. This was a completely new concept for me. I had always respected values such as courage and going on fighting even when the odds are against you.

But now I was being taught Christian values like humility and considering others better than myself. This went completely against the grain of the culture I had lived in.

For example, one day I was in the kitchen in the men's home, washing the dishes. I didn't mind that much. But then one of the guys who had been drying a very large cast-iron pan dropped it on my foot.

It hurt a lot, but he didn't apologize. Instead, he just quoted a scripture at me: "Consider yourself as nothing. Deny yourself!"

There were some sharp knives close by, and I considered putting one through his forehead.

He had forgotten who I was.

But God gave me the grace to be self-controlled and not to hurt him.

One thing I would not tolerate was hypocrisy. Every week we used to fast for one day, but one week I discovered a staff member secretly eating on our fast day! I was hungry, but had been asking the Lord to give me strength. Then to find this was too much. I challenged him to a fist fight.

"You're just a bunch of fakes and frauds," I declared.

So I left the rehab home for a month, although I continued to attend Sunday services at the local church with which the home was attached. I think I did this partly to show the guys at the home that I could make it as a Christian without them.

During this time I crashed my car. It was totally wrecked, but I walked away unhurt. Then I was riding my bicycle when two big dogs rushed out in front of me and made me swerve and fall off. I lay there stunned on the road, and the two dogs came and snarled at me threateningly. Fortunately their owner was nearby and called them off before they tore my throat out.

I could have been badly hurt or killed in both these incidents. God was protecting me. I repeatedly tried to get hold of a gun to use, but all my attempts failed.

I knew that God's hand was at work in it all – and that he was calling me back to full commitment to Him. But it was hard for me to humble myself, to admit that I had made a mistake and to return to the home.

I told Joe Lugo about the things which had been going on.

"You know what's happening, don't you?" he said. "The devil is trying to kill you. You're number one on his hit-list. He's the real assassin! Why don't you come back to the home?"

"I'll come back tomorrow."

"You might not be alive tomorrow."

One Friday Irene called on me. She said she wanted to know more about Christianity and asked if I would take her to church with me. We agreed to go together on Sunday.

But later that day a brother came to see me. After we had talked, he went to the bathroom, and he left an envelope of cocaine on the table. He hadn't left it for me, but I was tempted to use it. When he came back from the bathroom he caught me getting ready with my needle. He was surprised.

"Hey, Conejo, I thought you were a Christian now! Why are you using coke?"

"I am a Christian," I said, "but I need a break from it every now and then. It's no big thing."

He seemed disappointed. Part of him had seen some hope in

the fact that a Mafioso like me could become a Christian. "It's OK, you can keep the coke," he said, since he owed me money anyway.

Then he left.

I began to slam the coke, but I couldn't enjoy it. I was miserable.

By Sunday morning I was still high. Irene called around early to go to church with me, but as soon as I opened the door she could see that I was high. She was furious with me.

"How could you do this?" she said. "I believed all that stuff you told me about becoming a Christian! How dare you talk about God and the Bible? You're weak and you're a liar! I hate you! You're evil!"

I just stood there.

What could I say in my own defense?

I never saw her again.

I regret that very much. Who knows what could have happened if I hadn't let her down? She might have become a Christian, and our marriage might have come together again.

Since then she has remarried.

I still pray that she will come to know Jesus.

After almost four weeks I knew that I needed to go back to the home.

So I returned. Joe Lugo welcomed me back gladly. The first few days were difficult. By returning I had humbled myself, and that wasn't something I was used to doing.

As soon as I got back, I once again felt that peace in my heart which I had felt when I was converted. I knew I belonged there with those people. The other guys were very understanding and helpful.

"These things happen, Conejo, the same thing happened to me, but I came through it and came back to the Lord. Don't be too hard on yourself about it. You're just a baby Christian, and babies have a lot to learn!"

Above all I felt the love and mercy of God poured out on my

life.

Sometimes the home would run short of food, and we had to fast because there wasn't enough to eat! Then we would pray for God to meet our needs, and he always did. People would come around with boxes of food for us.

People kept telling me that my testimony was very powerful and was going to be used by God.

At first I didn't like to hear that word "testimony," because prior to becoming a Christian I had only heard it used in the context of court where someone was betraying his brother by giving a "testimony" to save his own skin.

It took me a while to understand that in the Christian context, a testimony was the story of how God had worked in someone's life.

Why had God saved me?

What purpose was there in it?

A recent Los Angeles district attorney's report estimates that there are 125,000 to 130,000 gang members in Los Angeles County. It makes no distinction between active, hard-core gang members and anyone who ever hung out with gang members, or was arrested once as a juvenile in the company of gang members, or even briefly flirted with joining a gang before pulling back.

"The reality of life in a gang-infested neighborhood is that every boy and girl must by necessity associate with gang members, because gang members are their classmates, their neighbors, their relatives. Though anxious parents have been known to bus their children to schools outside the neighborhood, sequestering them at home the rest of the time, these exceptions only prove the rule," wrote the *Los Angeles Times*.

How did we get to such a state of madness?

Many years ago, Chinese Communist Revolutionary Mao Tse Tung said that "true justice comes out of the barrel of a gun." Many people are living that today in America. For many, especially young African-American and Hispanic males in this nation's urban communities, their only source of power and self-esteem comes from a firearm.

Their only feeling of family comes from aligning with a gang.

Their only hope of rising out of poverty and shame is to beat the system – just as I tried.

The violence we witness is power. It is power that blames the victim for not cooperating with its evil intentions. It is power that justifies itself with a cold, conscienceless attitude that believes its victims deserve what they get.

It is easy to buy into the popular view that locking up criminals will keep us safe. Yet, we need to remember that more than 90 percent of the people currently in prison will be released. And I remember all too well how well I behaved each time they set me free.

We cannot do this thing in our own strength or in our own wisdom. The battle belongs to the Lord.

And the battle is raging.

The first form of combat in which you and I can effectively engage is on our knees. The Apostle Paul tells us in Ephesians 6:12, "For we wrestle not against flesh and blood, but against principalities, against powers, against the rulers of the darkness of this world, against spiritual wickedness in high places." I have learned that there is incredible truth in this verse. It is there, humbly approaching the throne of God that we can receive any marching order – if we are to enter the war in another way. It was on my knees that I received a great burden for the United Kingdom – England, Scotland and Wales – the island nation that birthed America's original thirteen colonies. You would think that, given my Hispanic heritage, the Lord would send me to Spain, the great nation that sent Columbus to discover the New World and which first colonized the lands of my forefathers. It would make even better sense to send me to Mexico.

But it is to England that I have been sent.

It amazes me, too.

Recently back in Los Angeles at a family reunion, I talked with kids who are my cousins and who I know are getting into the excitement of the violence all around them.

One of my cousins doesn't sell drugs or run guns or commit robberies.

"I just like hanging out with my friends," he told me quietly.

"I know," I told him, "but be careful."

My cousin saw a runaway girl's lifeless body blown away at a nearby telephone. He knows the deadly consequences of the streets. Only days later, a three-year-old girl walking home with her father and sister was killed in gang cross-fire.

Little three-year-old Denise Silva died while returning from the store in my Aunt Margaret's Boyle Heights neighborhood. The child was struck in the upper body by a bullet fired by a gang member who was aiming at somebody else, said Detective Robert Suter. Several young men armed with rifles and handguns opened fire at a group of people gathered on the sidewalk.

"It's sad. It's sad," said a neighbor. "It's a little girl, a little angel and they took her life. It's not right."

Then, as our neighborhood was still reeling from the tragedies, eleven-year-old Sabrina Haley was shot in the head in a drive-by shooting that occurred just minutes after local politicians, religious and community leaders began a news conference pleading for a halt to gang violence and a "killing-free" weekend.

"It's gotten absolutely nauseating," said Officer Steve Gross.

I told my cousin I don't want another kid in my family getting caught up in this madness. I wanted him to understand I have already lost too many people that I love.

It has taken the life of my half-brother Ralph.

It has snuffed out the incredible promise of my beloved Aunt Margaret's only son – the first member of the Blajos clan ever to go to college.

My cousins know not to brag to me about stalking rival gangs across railroad tracks and through alleys or of packing a *deuce-deuce,* a .22-caliber pistol. I might rage at them unexpectedly, tell them their adolescent game is so stupid – and that they are being used. East L.A. kids have been turned into small, vicious armies by drug profiteers' money. I know all too well.

Combat has changed from the bare knuckles of my childhood and the flashing knives of my adolescence to random shots at lookalike enemies who are blasted from a distance, faceless, unknown – gunned down without remorse as a rite of passage into manhood.

I was drawn by something called respect. They had power, too.

I wanted that.

I thought I had made the right choice.

I was wrong.

CHAPTER TWENTY

UP TO DATE

My older brother, Ernie, managed to escape the prison merry-go-round after doing five years for robbery. Though he went through various addictions, the fact that he fathered three beautiful children helped out. He surely would have returned to prison if he hadn't encountered the Lord in 1990 and went into one of our rehabilitation homes.

In June 1986, while I was still living in Visilia, my father had a massive heart attack. Seeing him strapped down in Los Angeles County Hospital with all sorts of tubes and wires numbed me. He was always so strong, in control.

"Why all the restraint?" I asked a nurse.

"George keeps pulling everything out, like he wants to die," she answered. "If he keeps it up the strain will kill him." For two days he wasn't responsive to the Gospel. On the third morning his deep blue eyes looked into mine and I knew he was open to what I had to say. He received the Lord and new life the day he died. I thank God for his great mercy.

In the early 1960s, the devil enlisted the cream of the crop of Californian Latinos, bringing death and terror. At about the same time, a young Sonny Arguinzoni began hitting the streets of Boyle Heights in East Los Angeles. The birth of another force came into the world – Victory Outreach. Everything I ever wanted in gang life – acceptance, family, brotherhood, a cause worth fighting for, a new identity, was in the Church of Victory Outreach.

Victory Outreach is tailor-made for the untouchable, rejects, drug addicts and prostitutes of the world's cities. It is an undeniable witness to all the world that Jesus Christ saves and transforms destroyed lives. Can you imagine the worst and most violent men of all races living together – not to mention praying together? Today there are over 10,000 men and women around the world in our rehabilitation homes.

After eleven months in a rehab home myself, I met evangelists Mando and Arlene Gonzales, who came to Visilia for a two-day crusade. Mando was from the old school of Southern California. We both knew many of the same people and developed a good rapport.

Mando asked me to pray about coming to the Mother Church in La Puente in order to receive further discipleship and direction. He even suggested going away with him on preaching engagements.

My pastor had no problem releasing me and I moved in with the Gonzales family, who lived near the church. This was the first time I had ever lived with a mature Christian family. Living with their three sons I realized how antisocial I really was. I now wonder how they put up with me.

Mando was the first to call me up to testify in front of two thousand people. I'll never forget how I was introduced.

"I have a very special brother with me I want to introduce to you. Please welcome Brother Art Blajos, a former assassin from the Mafia." I was shocked! To this day I don't know what I said.

In January 1988 I met Joey and Christina Rosales at a party at the home of Kathy Clark. Donald Garcia and myself were present. We had a profound impact on his life as we were both former members of the Mafia and were now serving God. Joey had been a leader in his local gang... Shortly after I met them, they both gave their lives to Christ. I have yet to witness as rapid a transformation as Joey's. Mando said of him, "I have never met anyone so much like Pastor Sonny as this young man. There is a heavy calling on his life. Watch over him." Mando took a personal interest in Joey and began speaking and demonstrating the dynamics of evangelism the Victory Outreach way.

I went up north to help Joe Lugo, who had become a pastor. When I returned to the Mother Church at La Puente I began to seriously think about going into Bible College full-time in order to be better equipped for the ministry. Thanks to Sam Sanchez, who was then the Vice President of the Latin American Bible College, I was able to enroll. I have never regretted my decision. Nicky Cruz of *The Cross and the Switchblade* and our own Pastor Sonny were two of the better-known alumni. At forty, however, I was one of the oldest guys there. I felt like a dinosaur!

In my second year the now Reverend Joey Rosales returned from Europe excited about a place in Wales called Cardiff. Apparently he accompanied Pastor Sonny, Mitchell Peterson, one of our Elders, and Pastor Brian Villalobos of London, England, on a tour. The next thing the new words around the church were "Wales for Jesus!" It was contagious. Joey, Christina and their three daughters moved there, and in an incredibly short time, he had a beautiful house, car, bus and rehab home with eleven men. A church was born.

A few years earlier, after listening to a sermon by Pastor Sonny on commitment, I walked over to him, looked calmly into his eyes and said "I'm with you until death. You can count on me." At the time I wasn't aware of the impact of what I said, but one thing I've learned about my pastor is that he has a great memory.

The Mother Church has thousands of members, so when the Senior Pastor notices you, that's a big event. Suddenly now, Pastor Sonny called me into his office. I tried to figure out what I had done wrong.

"Have you ever thought of going to England?"

"No, not really," I replied.

"Pastor Brian might be opening up a rehab home in Essex. Would you be open to that? At the same time you could check out Joey in Wales."

Pastor Sonny knew I was starting my second year in Bible

College, but he also knew I was losing interest in my studies. My grades and my discipline were excellent, but I knew my place was on the streets proclaiming the Gospel. I said I would be willing to do whatever it takes to establish our church anywhere, any time, any how, on the condition I could complete my degree when I returned to the States.

I thought I would return in six months.

So in February 1992 I arrived at King's Cross. When I first saw the devastation of sin there, I knew this was a Victory Outreach city. Drug addicts and crime were everywhere.

But the need in Wales was urgent. Joey had ten guys in a home and didn't know what to do with them all. We opened a rehab home in Pontypridd where I began to teach the biblical principles which have made this ministry successful around the world.

The church began to prosper, with up to forty people attending on Sundays. Then tragedy struck. Joey, a man of great energy and non-stop action, had leukemia. For him the pain of the disease was little compared to the burden he had for the souls of the men and women of Cardiff. Joey fought valiantly against incredible odds, but the killer disease took its toll. Christina spent her nights by his side at the hospital. I was certain they would pack up and fly back to the States, but Joey decided otherwise.

"I came to give my life for Wales and the vision of Victory Outreach. Either the Lord heals me or I die here in this country." Their dedication was an encouragement and a challenge to us all.

At the same time, many began to leave the church, confused about the future. Soon only a few remained. This was a time of testing and doubts. Why was God allowing this to happen to someone who loved him so much? Then I realized the Father knows a lot about losing a loved one. "He gave his only begotten Son... Unless a grain of wheat falls into the ground and dies..." I came to understand that Joey was definitely called and he was a precious seed that bore much fruit.

On September 8, 1993, in one of our largest memorial services ever, thousands came from all over the world to pay their respects and to comfort Joey's family. Christina and her beautiful daughters, Andrienna, Natosha and Olivette are now involved in ministry at the Mother church in La Puente. The best is yet to come for Victory Outreach, Wales.

After the funeral I returned to London along with a few others from Cardiff, under the leadership of Brian Villalobos. The church was meeting in King's Cross Road, a notorious part of London, and I was to help direct the men into the principles of discipleship and street evangelism. I soon discovered London to be more like Los Angeles than Cardiff. But city life is the same, sin is sin and a drug addict is the same the world over. I loved witnessing the grace of Jesus to hard-core addicts and violent criminals.

Tommy Jituboh was the main villain on "the Cross." They called him "the Governor." I liked Tommy immediately: he reminded me of myself in so many ways. He was one of the main drug connections.

With his mouth full of crack wrapped up in plastic, a can of beer in his hand, he was constantly smoking as he talked. He was an obvious leader, which I knew meant he had to be dangerous. I saw the wall of hate and defiance, a reckless bravado hiding the pain and despair. If ever a man was an impossible case, it was Tommy. But God specializes in impossible cases. My heart went out to him. More than that, I sensed the presence of God in a powerful way, and I said to myself, "It's a matter of time."

After months of prayer, believing that God would touch Tommy's heart, one afternoon I saw a young lady come into our coffee bar. She seemed so out of character for the area, I thought she was lost, but it turned out she was looking for me. God was on the move.

"Can you please help my brother Tommy?" she asked me.

"He's always going on about this bloke Art, and you're having quite an effect on his life."

That Sunday Tommy and his entire family came to church. They were trying to figure us out, making sure their brother wasn't joining up with a cult. We talked for a long time, and they were reassured that we were genuine. Tommy came into the rehab home telling us he was going to be violently sick in a few hours. He was addicted to heroin, methadone and the big one – cigarettes.

"You don't know how it is," he said. Junkies forget that we were once in their shoes.

"You don't know my God," I replied. That was in July 1993. Mr Jituboh is still waiting to go through drug withdrawal. Glory to God! Today Tommy is being groomed for the ministry sharing his incredible testimony all over the United Kingdom.

One day as we were preaching the Gospel at King's Cross, a broken and destitute man listened as he sipped his beer. At the end he came forward, reeking of alcohol, and weeping. Five years earlier he had been a successful businessman in India. After his business failed he escaped his many debts by coming to London, but he failed to get rich as he had planned, and became an alcoholic. When we met him, he believed he was a disgrace and would never see his wife and children again. That day God intervened and now the Reverend Tony Russell has begun Victory Outreach Madras, India.

Not all the men in Victory Outreach come from gang or drug related backgrounds. My friend Pastor Mike in Victory Outreach Church in Scotland was a police officer in London before teaming up with Pastor Brian. Another brother is working on his PhD, living in Durham.

The Victory Outreach Ministry in the Netherlands has grown in the past ten years to six churches: Amsterdam, Rotterdam, Den Helder, Den Haag, Lelystad and Utrecht. There are also two churches in Spain. I mention these churches because they offer me excellent opportunities as a visiting evangelist to impact these cities and to reach other "treasures out of darkness."

One night I was coming back from Walthamstow on the tube with a friend around 11 o'clock. Near us were eight or nine Asian and Black youngsters, and I began handing out some leaflets about my conversion. They crumpled them up and threw them on the floor. I didn't mind the literature being rejected: it comes with the territory. But too late I realized they were high on something, and one of them started picking a fight. In an instant, fists and feet were coming at us from all directions. The leader's fist came at me as if in slow motion. He had three or four large silver rings, and the impact on my face was explosive.

I felt the deadly rush of adrenalin flow through me. I became calm as I targeted his jaw to strike, grabbing his coat front pulling him towards my rising right hand intending to bust his jaw – then the inexplicable happened. My hand dropped and I just stood there taking their full assault. They stopped when they realized we were not fighting back, and the whole thing didn't last more than a minute and a half. We got off at King's Cross swollen, bloody and humiliated. Yet God had intervened and given me the strength to keep from doing what every cell in my body was crying out to do – destroy! What a deep change the Lord had worked within my heart. Truly I am a new creation.

These situations throw light on the reality of my conversion. I call them faith builders. It's hard work, but the rewards are immense.

While attending our International Spanish Conference in Mexico City where I was asked to speak, I was able to visit the pyramids of ancient Mexico – something I have always wanted to do. I was also honored to speak in front of 14,000 gang members from East Los Angeles, a few miles from my old neighborhood. It was a sight to see. Homeboys and homegirls were in full gang regalia, bald heads, scarred faces, tattoos everywhere. The best part of it was that ninety per cent of those youngsters were unsaved. At the end, thousands came forward and gave their lives to the King! It was one of the most memorable moments of my life.

There is no doubt in my heart that Victory Outreach International is poised to reach the world with the message that there is hope in Jesus Christ. We know in whom we believe and are confident that "United We Can."

In Christ

Art Blajos
London, England.

EPILOGUE

One cold January morning, I found myself looking at a picture of San Quentin State Prison where I was supposed to have died in the gas chamber. Two words came to mind: gratitude and power.

Some have asked me what gives me the right to speak publicly about my horrible and shameful past. My response is a command to preach the Gospel: "Go into all the world and preach the Gospel to every creature" (Mark 16:15).

I cannot change the past, but I can be an instrument that impacts the present with lasting effects on future lives. Nothing is more relative and powerful than a transformed man or woman living a holy lifestyle within the violent, crime-filled cities of the world. "I am not ashamed of the Gospel; it is the power of God unto salvation" (Romans 1:16).

Everywhere I go, I see "treasures out of darkness," which is to say, intelligent minds, courageous hearts, misplaced faith and shattered dreams rescued out of hopelessness and meaningless existence. I see the best and the brightest still covered by sin. They are diamonds in the rough, not doomed discards of society. At our Victory Outreach International World Conference in Long Beach, California, I saw 16,000 drug addicts, prostitutes, alcoholics and gang members from every nationality, from over 500 churches and rehabilitation homes. They were all under one roof, lifting their grateful, tattooed and scarred hands in triumph and praise to their Saviour Jesus Christ! This is real power. It is the reason I share my testimony.

I know the devastating effects of family and social rejection and finding a surrogate family in the barrio or gang.

Some think acceptance and protection are to be had in a new identity, as powerful bonds to the gang are developed. But it is a trap as they idolize the deceptive glamor of the gangster lifestyle. Our children sacrifice youth, strength and beauty to organizations that kill their own at the first sign of weakness – mental or physical. I was told that 90 percent of all gang members die young. Many are killed by drugs. Others spend years in and out of prisons.

For someone to become a hard-core member of organized crime is a process. It goes from a desire to being affiliated and grows into a yearning to be a hardened criminal. The sooner our young people see true Christian role models, the better. The challenge is for us to be those role models.

How can people like me, a former hitman, be any kind of a role model?

I can show kids that I was once like them. I have been there – and that I had to get out.

And that the only way out was Jesus Christ.

Nothing is impossible for God.

In the past years, we've seen a number of people transform their seemingly dead-end lives which were bound up by heroin, enslaved in prostitution, trapped in the lies of the criminal dream. I praise God for people such as Pete Stanislaus, Mandy Smally and Alex Newcome – just a few of the "treasures" under the guidance of Pastor Brian Villalobos, who also has established churches in Dublin, Ireland and Scotland, and Madras, India.

Once my life was in the Brotherhood. Today, I am proud to stand shoulder to shoulder with former member Donald Garcia, who is very active in the Church on the Way in Van Nuys, California, along with his lovely wife, Linda, and their children.

Juan Gonzales, another brother, is directing a rehabilitation home, The Ranch, in Helendale, California, along with his wife, Nina.

Beto Montellano, along with his wife, Yolanda, and son Danny, have directed homes in San Diego, California, and San Antonio, Texas. He is presently pioneering a men's home in Brixton, England.

And, praise God, one of the original founding members of the Brotherhood, a man I respect with all my heart, a man who spent forty years of his life in prison, surrendered to the King of Kings! Today Ernest "Kilroy" Roybal and his wife, Esther, and family are trophies of God's amazing grace. The conversion of Kilroy and the recent conversion of "Robot" Salas and his wife Rita refreshed my faith and confidence in the greatness of God.

Once upon a time, Kilroy and Donald Garcia were my mentors in death and destruction.

Today, together, we are bringing a message of life and hope for the glory of God and the salvation of many – and the vision of Victory Outreach!

AN INVITATION

At the start of this book I was under sentence of death. Apart from the blood of Jesus I still would be. So are you. Chains weighed me down. If you do not know Jesus, chains of sin still weigh you down.

Romans 10:9-10 tells us that if you confess with your mouth, "Jesus is Lord," and if you believe in your heart that God raised him from the dead, then you will be saved. "If the Son sets you free, you will be free indeed."

"How shall we escape if we neglect so great a salvation..." Hebrews 2:3

What will you do, my friend?

Choose life or death...Heaven or hell. I urge you to make a commitment to follow Jesus right now. Where you are. Please use this prayer.

Lord Jesus, I believe that you are the Son of God and that you died to save me. I want to be born again. Jesus, I ask you to forgive me for all my sins. I open my heart and invite you in to be my personal Lord and Savior. Amen.

For more information:

In the United States:
The Rev. Art Blajos
Victory Outreach Ministries International
P.O. Box 2748
La Puente, CA 91746

In Europe:
The Rev. Art Blajos
47 Forest Drive West
Leytonstone
London, E11 1JZ, England, UK